Understanding Strategy

GEOFFREY P. CHAMBERLAIN

ISBN: 1450517455
ISBN-13: 9781450517454
Library of Congress Control Number: 2010900352
CreateSpace, Charleston, SC

Contents

1
Introduction

The underlying premise of this book is that we often need to understand where some entity is going, and what path it will follow – in other words, its strategy. The uses of being able to analyze and understand strategy seem obvious. It can facilitate internal discussions between boards and chief executive officers (CEOs), and between CEOs and top teams. It can help insiders understand the context of their work, and let outsiders assess an organization's prospects. It can enable an organization's competitors to be more successful when game-playing with it, and allow its suppliers and customers to improve the outcomes of their dealings with it.

ANALYZING STRATEGY

My objective is to help readers understand any organization's strategy, and how it came to be adopted. Neither of these two matters—known as strategy content and strategy process[1]—can be truly understood without also understanding the other. There are two main reasons for this linkage. The first is reliability of perception; by knowing not just what, but also why and how, we gain the ability to make cross-checks on the validity of each point we think we understand. The second reason is improved predictive value; we are usually less interested in what the strategy is, than we are in what the organization will do next—which depends on how the strategist will interpret the strategy, and whether it will be modified or replaced. If we comprehend not only each aspect of the strategy, but also how the strategist thinks, how each aspect came into existence, and how these aspects are intended to take effect, there is some genuine depth to our perception; we have a multidimensional appreciation instead of just a flat-screen interpretation.

We could answer the what, why, and how questions about strategy by using a traditional case-study approach and describing the important aspects of the situation in detail. These reports do not enable us, though, to compare the strategies of different organizations.[2] We can make such comparisons much more easily if we identify the key features that characterize strategy, develop typologies for each, and carry out standardized analyses on the organizations of interest to us. We can then use the results to fit any organization into a context, giving us both a deeper perception and a better basis for predicting what it may do next. To acquire this capability we have to focus on how strategy works—and in particular on what shapes it, and what it fundamentally is. These matters are the subjects of the next two chapters. Each of the nine chapters that follow those two theory chapters analyzes the actual strategy of a real (but anonymous) organization.

WHAT IS STRATEGY?

Strategy is a social construct. Some other examples are thought, emotion, society, and law. Social constructs have no physically-demonstrable content and, therefore, mean whatever their users decide they should mean. If the concept definition is vague—as it usually is—there will be difficulties in building clear models or carrying out clear analyses. The strategy construct is a good example of the effects of lack of concept clarity. Users of the term commonly lack a specific view of what they mean by it, and often apply it to everything from broad-but-vague organizational sloganeering, to the almost-trivial.[3] The professional literature on strategy is similarly eclectic, and cannot even be characterized, except in terms of a number of individual streams.[4] Fortunately, the original foundational literature is rather more focused, and I will show in Chapter 3 that most of the influential definitions of strategy tend to be aligned with the direction-and-path concept.

The purpose of this book can only be satisfied by developing and applying a conception of strategy that is clear, specific, suited to modeling and analysis, and compatible with important sections of the strategy literature. The conception adopted in the book is derived and explained in Chapter 3. It is—by necessity—far more specific than any of those used by major literature branches, but its specificity is largely restricted to arbitrary structural rules that do not rely on any particular theory of how strategy is formed or takes effect. The book should, therefore, be applicable to analyzing any actual strategy, whether for an organization (business, government, military, religious, charitable, union, or social) or an individual person. However, for simplicity of expression, I will sometimes use business terms and leave readers to translate them appropriately for other applications.

A clear and specific strategy concept helps us analyze and understand real-world strategies, but does not constitute a set of instructions for forming them. In my experience, the people responsible for organizations' strategies often have no clearer conception of what the word means than other people do, but they are nevertheless often successful as strategists; being unable to describe an abstract concept does not always keep us from making constructive use of it. However having access to a clear concept and effective analytical tools can offer four practical benefits to strategists. First, it can enable them to recognize their own underlying assumptions and biases. Second, it can help them test the coherence of their strategies. Third, it can assist them in explaining their intentions to others, such as boards, investors, and financiers. Fourth, it can make them aware of how the final, implemented strategy differs from their conscious intentions, and how those differences arose.

This book is intended to assist not just strategists, but also anyone else who requires the ability to comprehend, explain, discuss, or criticize the coherence of an existing or proposed strategy. CEOs, board members, managers, and ambitious employees may want to apply this to their own organizations. Commentators, investors, members, and others may want to apply it to organizations of interest to them.

APPLYING THE THEORY: THE ALPHA CASE

The book is structured to develop the theory first, and apply it to actual case studies in subsequent chapters. However, to make it easier to follow the theory development, I have taken one of the ten case studies and used it as an example. The case—which I have called Alpha—will be described in this introductory chapter. In Chapters 2 and 3, as each section of the theory of strategy is developed, I will illustrate it by analyzing the corresponding aspect of the Alpha case. In all of the ten cases to be analyzed (including Alpha), the study-period is divided into two phases, with a substantial shift in the firm's strategic situation between the first and second. The second phase always ends at the time of the case study report.

The Alpha case concerns a man who worked in a high volume metal machining industry. This was a third tier supplier industry. It sold small, machined components to complex-component producers: a second tier industry. The complex-component producers assembled the parts they purchased to make complex components, which they sold to a first tier industry: finished goods producers such as automobile manufacturers. After fifteen years as an employee, the man decided to establish his own business in the same field. He began on a shoestring by borrowing from a finance company to buy a very small second-hand repetition-lathe, which he set up at home in his garage. His business was viable immediately, and after paying off the finance company, he bought four larger, but rather old and worn, automatic lathes, and operated them simultaneously in his garage. When he was out seeking orders or delivering components, his wife sometimes operated them. Over time he expanded, then developed a specific strategy that was substantially different from those of his competitors. At the time of the case study, twenty-one years after founding the business, he had about forty employees.

The First Phase: Getting the Business Started

There were two phases in Alpha's strategy development. The first was starting the business. The second, some years later, covered the emergence of a differentiated business strategy.

The CEO's decision to go into business was driven by three main factors. First, he disagreed with the management approach at the two similar businesses where he had worked. In particular, he strongly disapproved of the long-term "milking" of a business—that is, the majority of its earnings not being reinvested in the business itself. Second, his coworkers seemed unconvinced that he could succeed as a business owner, and he found this attitude galling. Third, he was personally ambitious.

It was evident to him that he would be financially exposed when he started the firm. He had a family and a mortgage, and to get started he had to quit his job and make a two-year commitment to a consumer finance company. At that time, his strategy was simple. First, he needed orders from customers, and his old employer's customers had assured him that they would give them to him. Second, he believed he could minimize initial risk by doing almost exactly what he knew his competitors were already doing. Third, he would strengthen and expand his business as quickly as possible. As a result of the second point, he started with old, worn machines, such as were usual in his industry at the time. As soon as his financial strength improved, he bought similar machines that were newly factory-refurbished. He could then meet the quality requirements of his customers—while his competitors were still following their traditional practice of hoping for the best and culling defective parts manually when necessary. This technically based conclusion that he could improve on what his competitors were doing was the first sign of his growing self-confidence. While the decision to adopt refurbished machines was not a strategic one—he made it clear it was done for operational reasons—it was the first indication of a practice of going his own way that would become highly evident in the second phase.

The Second Phase: Differentiation

After Alpha was on its feet and the CEO had some management experience, he was ready to exercise his own preferences more freely. The consequent revision of strategy was not due to the passage of time, or because he recognized that his first-phase strategy had become obsolete. The changes occurred progressively, but they were triggered by an event: the CEO suddenly had an inspiration. During a business trip to Japan, contrary to his previous attitude, he spontaneously became fascinated by a high technology computer numerically controlled machining center. In some brief period—perhaps a couple of days—while he watched it, examined it, and questioned user and vendor, he made an important tactical decision. He recognized that this machine could give his business a capability his competitors did not have. He immediately saw that this would enable him to access new component orders on which his main competitors could not even bid. Much later, the CEO identified this moment in Japan as a turning point in his business career. He bought the machine, and found that it did indeed help him win new contracts. He bought more high technology machining centers; in fact, they became the main type of machine he was buying. This eventually positioned Alpha as the high capability producer in its industry segment.

While this trend was emerging, he took other steps that also differentiated his company. He found that his customers often needed to shorten their lead time between ordering machined metal components, and receiving them in large quantities. His solution once again was technology-based. He reasoned that if he bought a high technology "wire-cutting" electrical discharge machining center, he could make his job-specific cutting tools in his own factory instead of ordering them from specialist tool-making firms. This would shorten lead time on new product orders by several weeks. It would also improve his reliability as a supplier, since he could produce new cutting tools within half an hour to replace broken ones. In parallel with this, he began approaching customers with alternative designs for their products' components. He offered the new versions at lower cost but with the same functionality as their own designs.

All of these changes—which cumulatively created a differentiated approach to the market based on superiority in technology and service—were partly the result of his personality. As an ego-driven individual who was enthusiastic about technology, he found this to be a way to make his own skills, decisiveness, and risk-tolerant nature into central features of his business.[5]

NOTES

1. See Fahey (1986) and Huff and Reger (1987) for details regarding this traditional distinction in the literature.

2. Readers with a background in methodology will be aware that comparing the contents of multiple case studies raises some epistemological issues. I will address this point briefly, and give a reference explaining my solution, in Chapter 3.

3. I recall one CEO adding the word "strategic" to the existing names of his various top-team meetings.

4. Mintzberg, Ahlstrand and Lampel (1998) offer a potentially useful suggestion as to how the literature can be subdivided into themes to improve its accessibility. I will make use of that approach at times in this book.

5. Alpha's strategy involved a higher risk-profile than its competitors' due to the greater financial exposure caused by the need to pay for expensive machines. Its fixed costs were higher, so the factory had to run consistently at high production volumes. (Fixed costs are those that continue whether or not the company produces anything. Essentially, these are the costs of the factory, management, machinery, tooling, and facilities being there, ready to produce components. It excludes variable costs of production, which are proportional to output, not independent of output.)

2
The Forces That Shape Strategy

Strategy is shaped by two types of forces: the organization's environment, and the strategist's personality. The first environmental force any organization has to address is its underlying purpose: a direction imposed by the members or owners, and intended to guide the entity's actions. This intention is determined, and to the extent possible enforced, by those who theoretically have ultimate control of the organization—perhaps its owners, its external members, or its electors. Initially selecting an underlying purpose that will attract support is usually one of the key functions of an organization's founder. To accomplish the underlying purpose, those guiding the organization have to deal with various other environmental forces—such as the positions and actions of customers, employees, competitors, suppliers, and regulators. All of these forces can to some extent be overridden, circumvented, reshaped, stretched, or manipulated by the organization's own actions. However doing so takes time, effort, risk, and resources, and in most practical cases, all of these are in limited supply. The purpose of strategy is to maximize the extent to which the organization achieves its underlying purpose.[6] Forming strategy consists of finding a general approach to achieving this, then choosing ways to deal with the environmental forces so that as much progress as possible can be made.

To set the scene for describing strategy in Chapter 3, this chapter outlines and categorizes the forces that organizations may use in achieving their underlying purposes. The organization and its environment impinge on each other in many ways. Strategy succeeds or fails by interacting with this environment. It succeeds by avoiding, making use of, or overcoming, the impingements. A rudimentary typology of aspects of the environment is useful in describing both how the environment may impede strategy, and how a specific strategy is to take effect.

THE ENVIRONMENT

Dividing the Environment into Categories

Analyzing, describing, and comparing strategic options are easier if we assign the key issues to categories, rather than dealing with them in individual detail. Therefore, I will arbitrarily divide the organization's entire environment into three basic categories. First, there is the area outside the organization, which I will call the *external environment.* Some important opportunities to achieve underlying purposes are external, for example, influencing customers, competitors, supply and distribution chains, opinion-leaders and critics, and legislators and regulators. Second, there is the area inside the organization, which I will call the *internal environment.* Strategy can succeed by applying internal forces, for example, dominating the supply of key resources such as raw materials or intellectual property, or making the organization more effective and efficient than its competitors through superior skills, morale, financial strength, or facilities and equipment. Third, there is the organization's *shareholder* group, a special category intermediate between the external and internal environments. It consists of the organization's external members and their proxy, the board of directors. The purpose of strategy—maximizing the extent to which the underlying purpose is achieved—can be partly satisfied by influencing the group that has the power to determine the underlying purpose. If shareholders can be persuaded, for example, to accept more risk or lower returns, management's task becomes easier. The purpose of strategy is to maximize the alignment between the outcome and the underlying purpose. This can be done by changing either the outcome or the purpose; there is no rule that says strategy can only change the outcome.

Dividing Influence-Techniques into Categories

If the purpose of strategy is maximizing the achievement of the underlying purpose, and this depends on how the organization deals with its environment, we need to consider the basic, generic mechanisms by which strategy can influence this environment. For convenience, we can use a single, simple dichotomy for this. One of the two well-known generic influence-techniques involves assuming that human beings are completely *rational* creatures whose actions are guided by the logical principles of economics, and in particular by utility theory and games theory.[7] The alternative generic approach is asserting that humanity is not entirely rational and, therefore, can sometimes be persuaded by alternative techniques based on principles of psychology, including manipulation of emotion, self-esteem, and social dynamics. This *social* view does not exclude the rational view; it merely asserts that an assumption of perfect rationality will often give the wrong answer, and is not the best option to choose.[8]

Environmental Forces in the Alpha Case

As explained in Chapter 1, in the first phase of the Alpha case, a skilled tradesman decided to found his own metal-machining business. His reasons were dominated by his personality. At first he was critically short of two essential resources: money and business skills. Accordingly he adopted a defensive posture—emulating his competitors—for as short a time as possible, until he saved some money and acquired some experience. As soon as he could, he began to depart from the usual behavior of his competitors and express his own personality. This tendency became highly pronounced in the second phase of the case. Thus two environmental factors shaped Alpha's first-phase situation, and therefore its strategy. The first of these—a severe shortfall in internal resources—applied only for the first few years, because the CEO made it his main priority to overcome it. The second factor, which increasingly became dominant, was the CEO's way of thinking. In the second phase the entire strategy was dominated by this factor.

THE STRATEGIST

The purpose of this chapter is to explain the forces that shape strategy. Up to now, I have focused on environmental forces, many ich support or constrain achieving the organization's underlying purpose. The rest of the chapter will be directed toward the other force that shapes strategy: the thoughts of the strategist; that is, the person or group making the organization's strategic decisions. Because strategic choices are made by human beings, they are products not only of input data (the environment), but also of cognitive processes (the way data are analyzed and evaluated to produce a decision). Unless the people who make these decisions are perfect examples of the legendary Rational Man, the outcome will be influenced to some extent by various distortions and emphases, which I will call *cognitive bias.* The literature gives several specific but widely-differing accounts of how strategists think, which suggests that while approaches to strategy formation vary, they may nevertheless tend to fall into a few distinct types. A typology of cognitive biases that accounts cumulatively for the majority of strategists, and is based on stable, preferably testable, psychological preferences is potentially a powerful tool for analyzing and understanding strategy.

The Underlying Concept

Management literature contains insightful descriptions of some specific types of decision-makers.[9] It also offers at least one general model of decision-makers based on factors said to influence their ways of thinking.[10] However, it does not, as far as I know, supply a model of strategists' cognitive biases based on recognized psychological concepts and capable of supporting a typology.[11] Nevertheless the literature does provide powerful clues. Alfred Chandler Jr. found that some strategists readily accepted major change, while others were reluctant—and this had a crucial effect on the strategies they chose.[12] Kenneth Andrews' description of strategy formation referred to three different motivations that he believed should, and do, influence strategists.[13] These were pursuing economic success, implementing the strategist's own desires, and creating benefits for society.[14] Combining these two concepts, strategists' decisions seem to be substantially influenced by two psychological factors. The first is whether the person is or is not receptive toward major change. I will call this factor *change-readiness,* which is one of the elements of cognitive style. The second factor is motivation: the way each person balances three basic objectives when making decisions. I will call this factor *cognitive emphasis.* The professional literature provides some

other support for a typology using change-readiness and cognitive emphasis as the bases for a two-factor model of cognitive bias.[15] Implementing the typology requires selecting specific, established psychological variables to describe these two factors.

Change-Readiness

Having selected change-readiness as the first measure in the cognitive bias typology, we now require a recognized psychological measure of it. Michael Kirton reported on a stable cognitive style preference regarding change-readiness.[16] He called those who prefer incremental change, or modifying what has gone before to remedy its deficiencies, *adaptors*. He called those who prefer discontinuous change, or discarding what has gone before and starting again, *innovators*.[17] Appendix 1 lists out a number of characteristic differences between adaptors and innovators that have been reported in the professional literature. Most people are located fairly close to the midpoint of the scale and only exhibit these characteristics as a mild tendency.

Adaptive and innovative strategists can be expected to think and act differently. Adaptors, or change-conservatives, are biased toward gradual, low-risk progress concentrating on near-term issues. Their desires for stability and low risk lead them to regard the traditional configurations of their organizations as policies, and they are reluctant to review them. For the same reasons they prefer to deal with observed organizational imperfections incrementally through tactical or operational decisions. They address unusual threats or opportunities only when they become clearly visible.[18] Innovators are biased toward change and are ready to accept some risk. They are fairly comfortable with unstructured, unclear, and ambiguous situations; tend to act impulsively; and are impatient with detail. Innovators are less concerned than adaptors about achieving consensus, complying with constraints, respecting tradition or limiting disruption. They also de-emphasize the immediate outcome in favor of the long-term.[19] They, therefore, are likely to regard strategic thinking as a natural and necessary undertaking.

Cognitive Emphasis

A suitable typology of cognitive emphases would make use of an established psychological measure that identifies the three motivations Andrews said were relevant to strategists. I have found only one such measure: Eduard Spranger's six "types of men."[20] His theory asserts that each type has its own single, stable, primary motivation.[21] Three of these types—those he called economic, political and social—are closely aligned with the three motivations identified by Andrews. People conforming to the remaining three types seem less likely to be successful as key strategic decision-makers in organizations engaged in competition. Spranger regarded the economic, political, and social types as action-oriented, but he described each of the other three—theoretic, aesthetic and religious—as primarily motivated to bring about a personal mental experience rather than a physical outcome.

Spranger said that the theoretic type (or theorist) "has become, so to speak, all objectivity, necessity, general validity and applied logic." The result is that people of this type tend to disregard practical considerations. "But no other side of existence is to him so unimportant subjectively, as these immediate needs.... The necessary consequence is that in the face of the practical problems of life the pure theorist is helpless."[22] He said that the aesthetic type (or aesthete) emphasizes sensory experiences "with a minimum of logical reflection."[23] As a result, "the aesthetic man is as indifferent and helpless in the face of the practical demands of life as the theorist".[24] He based his description of the religious type (or mystic) on two propositions. First, "God is the objective principle which is thought of as the object of the highest personal value experience."[25] Second, "a religious man is he whose whole mental structure is permanently directed to the creation of the highest and absolutely satisfying value experience."[26] He reasoned that these propositions have consequences for mystics' perceptive processes. "The cognition of reality is discontinued and a higher logic introduced whose truth is to be understood purely religiously."[27] Thus Spranger asserted that the primary motivations of members of the three contemplative types do not drive them to undertake real-world activities. He understood that they do undertake such activities, but he believed that this is a result of secondary and even lower-order motivations.

It is reasonable that a simple, parsimonious typology of strategists based on Spranger's theory should be restricted to primary preferences and, therefore, include only the three action-oriented types. Secondary motivations may sometimes cause physical actions; theorists may found technology companies, aesthetes art galleries, and mystics religions, but the theory tells us that the organizations concerned are only of secondary importance to their founders—which is likely to have important practical effects. Spranger said that when lesser motivations conflict in any way with a person's primary motivation they "are repressed to utter meaninglessness."[28] Disregarding secondary motivations not only simplifies the typology, it also reconciles it with Andrews, who considered only the three action-oriented cognitive emphases to be relevant to deliberate strategic decision-making for organizations.

Spranger's typology is derived from theory, is long-established and somewhat specific, and is suited to providing a single-term description of a stable dominant motivation. However, we need more specific type descriptions if we are to make the typology useful for the purposes of this book.[29]

Spranger said the *economic* type always uses utility as the preferred value[30]—or in other words is motivated by economic issues and concerns. This aligns well with the economic motivation asserted by Andrews.[31] The first type, therefore, will be called the *materialist*, field-identified by two characteristics. First, the creation of personal and organizational economic benefits is given a higher priority than personal empowerment or aggrandizement. Second, the views and interests of external groups, including the general community, are considered strategic issues if the groups may otherwise eventually threaten organizational economic benefits.

Spranger said of the *political* type, "The purely political type makes all value regions of life serve his will to power."[32] He also said of this type, "... our goal (power) is the highest value and as such is beyond all discussion."[33] Consequently, I will define the acquisition and exercise of power as the imperative for the second type. This is similar to the motivation to exercise personal will that Andrews described.[34] I will call this type the *egotist*, and field-identify its members by two features. First, such people seek to possess and exercise the power to make important decisions personally, arbitrarily, without review, and in most cases, visibly. Second, they treat pursuing personal emphases and goals as primary, with the interests of other parties—including the organization itself and the public—given lower priority.

Spranger said that the *social* type sees other people as the ultimate repository of value.[35] Value, therefore, is maximized by advancing the interests of the human species or specific groups or members of it. This third type aligns with the social accountability motivation described by Andrews.[36] I will call the type the *altruist*, and field-identify members by two characteristics. First, they make decisions primarily for the benefit of some group that may have no direct connection with the organization. The interests of the organization and its shareholders or controlling members may be seen as legitimate, but secondary compared with the imperative need to serve the target group. Second, they may evaluate benefits using broader measures than materialistic ones.

Six Types of Strategist

Combining the two approaches to change and the three cognitive emphases, we can describe six types of strategist.

The *adaptive materialist* is focused on creating economic value without risk or disruption—and preferably without making decisions on issues such as the organization's basic configuration. Long-term commitments are only made when they are necessary and the picture has become somewhat clear. Decisions are approached with a focus on *the organization itself.* Because of the adaptors' emphasis on consensus, the top teams' acquiescence in important decisions may be treated as a step in the decision-process itself rather than as part of the implementation phase. The adaptive materialists' strategy is largely short-term and reactive, constituting mere tactical responses by Andrews' standards, so success is primarily determined by the quality of their performance as executive managers. The characteristic behavior of taking recurrent small bites at improving the organization's performance, with narrowly-focused, carefully-managed upheavals when clearly necessary, has led me to call this type *Executives.*

The *adaptive egotist*, as an egotist, wants to exercise power by making arbitrary decisions, but as an adaptor is reluctant to make truly strategic decisions, preferring a short-term focus. Indeed to adaptive egotists even tactical decisions are unattractive because each of them constrains a series of subsequent operating decisions, whereas egotists require freedom to act powerfully and arbitrarily at all times. Decisions are approached in terms of *making the deal.* Adaptive egotists like to make operating decisions themselves, so they prefer to avoid delegating authority or establishing rules or procedures that might subsequently constrain them personally. The lack of strategic and tactical engagement, which results in a primary focus on operating decisions, led me to name this type *Operators.*

The *adaptive altruist* aims to generate advantages—and prevent disadvantages—for some group or social cause. Decisions are approached with the objective of *delivering a specific social benefit.* In the context of a commercial organization, while shareholders' right to a return on investment may be recognized, it is not seen as primary. Instead, shareholders are seen as one of a number of constituencies to be addressed and managed.[37] Like all adaptors, this type desires inclusion in a group consensus, and can feel isolated in commercial organizations where a materialistic or egotistic motivation may be more usual. I will call the type *Administrators.*

The *innovative materialist* wants to maximize economic value created and is likely to use a fresh or sometimes even a unique viewpoint. Decisions are focused on a *visualized concept of the organization.* Major change—even of business configuration—is not regarded negatively, risk is managed rather than avoided, and because of high self-confidence, after forming a strategic vision members of this type may see any top-team resistance to it as a strategy implementation issue rather than a reason to question the vision itself. They dislike detail and prefer to delegate management of it. In view of the emphasis on where the organization should go rather than where it is now, and on large long-term economic gains rather than avoiding short-term risk and disruption, I have called innovative materialists *Pioneers.*

The *innovative egotist* combines egotists' desire for power and freedom from constraints, with innovators' desire for change. Decisions are seen in terms of pursuing a *visualized opportunity.* As egotists, they want to possess and exercise power without oversight or delegation. As innovators, they emphasize long-term gains rather than short-term ones, willingly embrace risk, and are impatient with detail. Because of the conflicting desires to avoid both delegation and detail, administrative issues may be pseudo-delegated; arbitrary reversal of delegated decisions may occur. The innovators' impulsiveness interacts with the egotists' desire to exercise power, and may result in a succession of visions, each of which they pursue emphatically. They are not overly concerned with foolish consistency; when a new vision arises, existing strategy—and perhaps commitments—may quickly be over-ridden. In view of their preoccupation with vision, power, and risk, I have called them *Entrepreneurs.*

The *innovative altruist,* as an altruist, wants to create greater benefits for some social group, and as an innovator, is focused on long-term gains while having neither regard for consensus nor interest in detail. This may result in a large gap between the chosen strategy and the views of various stakeholders. Members of this type approach decisions in terms of *creating a visualized social improvement.* This imperative demand for remarkable solutions to a challenging or even conflicting set of objectives suggests a name for innovative altruists: *Visionaries.*

Using the Cognitive Bias Model

There are long-established, objective psychological tests for both the change-readiness and cognitive emphasis parameters for the typology.[38] In practice, however, strategy practitioners and researchers may often need to make subjective assessments.[39] This seems quite practical provided the assessor is familiar with the concepts and with the people being assessed.[40]

The typology of strategists does not apply universally. While Andrews referred approvingly to three motivations, he did not claim that they are the only ones that can exist,[41] and Spranger's theory asserts that there are six possible types of motivation rather than just three. However, the typology is useful if the six types it describes (three kinds of adapters and three kinds of innovators) collectively account for a substantial majority of real-world strategists. Both reasoning and various indications in the literature suggest that this is likely. A very small-scale test of its usefulness can be inferred from the ten case analyses in this book.

Classifying Alpha's Strategist

The typology of strategists is based on change-readiness (whether the strategist was adaptive or innovative) and cognitive emphasis (the strategist's primary motivation—usually materialistic, egotistic or altruistic). The strategist's cognitive bias—the combination of these two characteristics—is thus expected usually to fall into one of six categories. Our next step is to classify Alpha's strategist, the firm's founder and CEO.

Change-Readiness

A simple set of field-identifiable distinctions between adaptors and innovators was set out earlier in the chapter. Essentially, adaptors prefer incremental change (adapting what came before) while innovators prefer discontinuous change (replacing what came before). Furthermore, adaptors prefer to avoid or minimize risk, while innovators tend to be impulsive and regard a degree of risk as an inevitable and appropriate accompaniment to desirable change.

The Alpha CEO had worked in the mass-production metal-machining industry, as apprentice then as journeyman, before starting his own similar business. After a cautious, low technology strategic stance copied from his competitors in the first phase, he visited Japan and was captivated by a new high technology machine costing perhaps ten times as much as anything he had at the time. His enthusiasm for the machine led him to make an immediate decision to buy it.[42] His explanation demonstrated his impulsiveness.[43] Having bought the machine, he used it to capture additional business, liked the results, and bought more machines with the same technology. The sudden decision to buy the first high technology machine is the key to identifying the Alpha CEO's change-readiness. He instantly recognized a potential, and committed himself to investing in new technology that his competitors did not have. This was not a result of environmental pressure; there was no threat to his firm at the time. He simply saw an opportunity and pursued it, despite commercial and financial risk, disruption, pre-existing personal apprehension about the technology involved,[44] and the potential need for cultural change in his company. Unless this was an anomalous act, he, therefore, must have been an innovator. Looking at other circumstances though, we also find his decision to use refurbished machines when competitors used worn-out ones, his unconventional practice of offering alternative designs to customers without being asked, and his purchase of an automated electrical discharge machining device to provide a lead time advantage, despite having to break the prevailing paradigm in the process.[45] These choices support the initial indication that he was distinctly an innovator, not an adaptor.[46]

Cognitive Emphasis

We distinguish between materialists, egotists, and altruists by identifying which of three objectives is treated as a strategic imperative and, therefore, always ranks ahead of other considerations.[47] For a materialist the imperative is to maximize income. For an egotist it is to maximize the power to make arbitrary decisions. For an altruist it is to maximize benefits for society or some section of society.[48]

There are four main indications of the Alpha CEO's preference. First, his most prominent reason for starting his own business was that he wanted a challenge.[49] Second, as soon as possible after starting the business, not only did he begin to make his decisions personally using his own subjective criteria, but also he reveled in this and wanted it to be widely known that he did so.[50] Third, he liked to make on-the-spot decisions without analysis.[51] Fourth, he structured his business practices—which ultimately shaped his firm's strategy—so that he was at the center of events, always relevant and always making powerful decisions.[52] These behaviors match the characteristics of an egotist.[53]

Cognitive Bias

Putting the change-readiness together with the cognitive emphasis, we find that the Alpha CEO was an *innovative egotist*—the type I have dubbed the *Entrepreneur.* The type description given earlier in this chapter fits him very well. When he first saw a new computer numerically controlled machining center in Japan, he made an immediate decision that later turned out to have strategic implications.[54] His explanation of this abandonment of his previous defensive strategy highlighted his impulsive, powerful style.[55] This event marked the beginning of the second phase and along with other changes, gradually differentiated him as the high capability, high service level competitor in his industry segment. He always had a vision, and pressed forward powerfully toward it.[56] The vision was always his, and he had no qualms about changing it when a better vision occurred to him.[57] He appears to have done little or no genuine delegating of authority in matters that were significant to him,[58] and felt free to intervene suddenly, arbitrarily and decisively whenever and wherever he chose. His firm's strategy and posture were more aggressive and riskier than those of its competitors.[59] His own profile was high, and his visibility was centered on matters that were important to him.

NOTES

6. Actual outcomes depend not only on what the organization sets out to do (its strategy) but also on how well it implements the strategy.
7. This is the conceptual basis of the economic model Adam Smith introduced in 1776 (Smith 1991). It is commonly called the Rational Man or Economic Man ("Homo economicus") model.
8. Because the classification is structured as a dichotomy, every influence technique must belong to one class or the other. Thus, on one side there is an assumption of perfect rationality, and on the other side, bounded (i.e., partial) rationality supplemented by psychological factors.
9. See for example Cyert and March (1963) and Kets de Vries (1977).
10. (Hambrick and Mason 1982).
11. Donald Hambrick and Phyllis Mason (1982) wrote a well-known paper aimed at identifying the source of the individual differences between leaders. However, for practical reasons based on distinctions between professions and types of professional literature, they avoided psychological concepts and classified decision-makers in terms of their basic demographics, though they admitted the limitations of this approach. I will take a step beyond Hambrick and Mason by making some minimal use of two established psychological measures.
12. (Chandler 1962). Chandler studied the transitions of some of America's largest corporations from centralized, functional structures to decentralized, market-driven structures. He concluded that this transition alleviated the past problem of administrative issues causing diseconomies of scale in a number of very large functionally-structured organizations. He also observed that in specific cases, the structural transition could not occur until certain executives retired and were replaced by others with different approaches. The new leaders "considered their problems to be administrative rather than functional ones, to be answered by new organizational structure and practice" (1962 p. 381). Chandler's favorable view of the change-ready leaders was similar to Andrews' (1971) and Kenichi Ohmae's (1982) approaches to strategy formation. Other classic literature described and justified the opposite, or change-averse, style of strategist (Lindblom 1959; Cyert and March 1963; Quinn 1978).
13. (Andrews 1971). This text became the basis for a major stream of literature known as the Design School (Mintzberg et al. 1998 p. 24). Note that Andrews' text also formed the text portion of the various editions of Learned, Christensen, Andrews and Guth (1965), Christensen, Andrews and Bower (1973), and Christensen, Andrews, Bower, Hamermesh and Porter (1987).

14. He generally prescribed an economic emphasis (1971 p. 37), but included two chapters taking different positions. In Chapter 4 (1971 pp. 103-117), he explained that strategists' decisions must reflect their own views and desires. In Chapter 5 (1971 pp. 118-177), he asserted that companies must take account of social obligations. Andrews' three motivational streams are supported respectively by the economic literature (Porter 1985; Teece, Pisano and Shuen 1997), the psychological branch of the entrepreneurial literature (Kets de Vries 1977; Busenitz and Barney 1997), and the social accountability branch of the stakeholder literature (Lindblom 1959; Barnett 2007).

15. There is direct empirical evidence supporting the relevance of this simple two-factor cognitive-emphasis-plus-change-readiness model of cognitive bias. Shalom Schwartz (1992) developed from theory, a survey of personal values containing ten items. He validated his construct empirically using intercorrelation analysis of his research data. This analysis led Schwartz to observe that his ten values could be visualized as addressing just two mutually-independent higher-level dichotomies: self-enhancement versus self-transcendence (selfishness versus altruism); and openness to change versus conservation (change-readiness). Schwartz's altruism motivation appears to correspond with Andrews' (1971 p. 118) and Charles Lindblom's (1959) social accountability motivation. His change-readiness concept seems aligned with the dimension implicitly revealed above by comparing Chandler's two strategist types: those who changed their firms' structures to suit their strategies, and those who were reluctant or even unwilling to reconsider their business structures. This change-readiness dimension is further clarified by considering Norman Smith's (1967) finding (by analyzing data from Collins, Moore and Unwalla (1964)) that there were two distinct types of business founder. Both types were motivated by the desire to act out their personal wills, which aligns with Andrews (1971 p. 103) and Maynard Kets de Vries (1977). One type, dubbed opportunistic, displayed a proactive, change-ready style. The other type, termed craftsman, was conservative and defensive.

16. (Kirton 1976). In another important paper, Danny Miller, Manfred Kets de Vries, and Jean-Marie Toulouse (1982) found a connection between chief executives' locus of control (Rotter 1966) and their firms' innovation, risk taking, proactiveness, and futurity—all of which can be related to change-readiness versus conservatism (Kirton 1976). While this is additional evidence of the relevance of change-readiness to strategists' behavior, locus of control is not a suitable psychological measure of change-readiness because it is partly a situational variable. It, therefore, does not report on a stable preference. Schwartz's (1992) change-readiness dimension, previously described, is also inadequate for the proposed typology because it is not supported by extensive detail or literature.

17. Kirton's measure—the Kirton Adaption-Innovation Inventory (KAI)—is determined by a standardized, validated and well-known test instrument

(Kirton 1976), and is supported by a stream of literature (Foxall and Payne 1989; Kirton 1989; Buttner and Gryskiewicz 1993; Clapp 1993; Taylor 1994; Chan 1996; Mudd 1996). There is also evidence that subjective estimates of this measure made by people moderately familiar with it and with a test subject typically yield useful indications (Kirton and McCarthy 1985). This is a desirable feature for field applications, given the likely resistance of many strategists to undertaking psychological tests (Hambrick and Mason 1982). Although KAI is a single continuous variable on which the human population is normally-distributed, for the purposes of this book, strategists will be described as adaptors if they are on the adaptive side of the population mean and innovators if on the innovative side.

18. Such responses are the adaptors' form of strategy, and align well with descriptions in the literature on change-averse strategists (Lindblom 1959; Cyert and March 1963; Quinn 1978).
19. This aligns well with the concept of deliberate strategy formation implicit in the Design school of literature (Mintzberg et al. 1998 p. 24) exemplified by Chandler (1962), Andrews (1971 pp. 27-30) and Ohmae (1982).
20. Eduard Spranger (1928) developed by reasoning, the concept that there are six generic types of people, each based on a specific cognitive emphasis. He named the types theoretic, economic, aesthetic, social, political, and religious. Subsequent to publication of Spranger's book, a questionnaire instrument nominally based on his six types came into regular use (Allport and Vernon 1930).
21. Spranger emphasized that just one of the six motivations permanently dominates each person's thinking, and while all of the other five motivations are also present, when they would conflict with the dominant motivation they "are repressed to utter meaninglessness. We may symbolize this in the figure of a gambler's die, of which in every instance one side with its figures must lie uppermost. The others are not, however, absent but are instead in a definite relation to the figures on top" (1928 p. 104).
22. (Spranger 1928 p. 112).
23. (Spranger 1928 p. 149).
24. (Spranger 1928 p. 154).
25. (Spranger 1928 p. 211).
26. (Spranger 1928 p. 213).
27. (Spranger 1928 p. 225).
28. (Spranger 1928 p. 104).
29. Strategists in real organizations may be unwilling to undertake psychological tests (Hambrick and Mason 1982), so for the new typology to be fully

useful, the types must be identifiable by subjective observations in the field. This requires specific type-descriptions. To prevent confusion with Spranger's philosophical descriptions of his six types, I will rename the three relevant types on the basis of the primary decision criteria they use.

30. (Spranger 1928 p. 132).
31. (Andrews 1971 p. 37). This motivation has been central to economic models since Adam Smith's in 1776 (Smith 1991 p. 20), including Michael Porter's analyses (1980; 1985).
32. (Spranger 1928 p. 190).
33. (Spranger 1928 p. 192).
34. (Andrews 1971 p. 103). Much the same point was made by Kets de Vries (1977) and Norman Smith (1967).
35. (Spranger 1928 p. 173).
36. (Andrews 1971 p. 118). It was also central to Lindblom (1959) and is one of the motivations (self-transcendence) Schwartz (1992) detected by reviewing intercorrelation analysis of his human values research data.
37. This is the ongoing political process modeled by Charles Lindblom (1965 p. 3).
38. Gordon Allport and Philip Vernon (1930) published a test instrument intended to establish subjects' types in accordance with Spranger's typology. See Vernon and Allport (1931) for additional details. The instrument was later updated (Allport, Vernon and Lindzey 1960) and has been used extensively in career-choice counseling. Kirton's (1976) test instrument is also in common use by psychologists.
39. This is because strategists may often be unwilling to submit to psychological tests.
40. As noted above, Kirton and McCarthy (1985) found that under such circumstances subjective estimates provide useful indications of change-readiness. Spranger's typology was designed in the first place to be assessed subjectively.
41. Andrews (1971 p. 106) was aware, at a minimum, of Spranger's theorist type. The literature suggests that Andrews' report on a theorist who had founded a business to manufacture his own inventions may not have been an isolated case. Norman Smith (1967 pp. 87-89) observed that ten of his fifty-two business founders did not fit either his opportunist or craftsman type, but seemed to fit an inventor type.
42. From an interview with the CEO and general manager (subsequent notes also are from the interview).

CEO: I've been over to Japan many years ago and walked in and saw the machine and I've just thought "Wow, I've never seen anything like this in Australia." And bought it straight there off them.

43. Interviewer: When you decide this machine can do something for me, and this other machine can't?

CEO: Yep.

Interviewer: How long does it take you to figure that out?

CEO: Thirty seconds.

Interviewer: Right. And how do you do it?

CEO: Make a decision.

Interviewer: But what do you put into the decision?

CEO: My thought.

44. CEO: I think initially when we started we were in multi-spindle lathes, which is the ones behind me. There's a (press article) where I was quoted as saying CNC, computer numerical control technology, scared the crap out of me. I didn't want to get involved.

Interviewer: Because you wouldn't have the technology to support it?

CEO: Yes. I was very much afraid of it.

45. The convention in the high-volume metal-machining industry was that only the larger companies had any in-house tool-making capability, and even those firms purchased some of their tooling. All tooling for small firms was made by highly-skilled specialist suppliers. After he obtained the EDM machine, however, the Alpha CEO had most of his specialized cutting tools designed, programmed, and made in-house in a few days instead of several weeks. Replacement tools could then be produced in twenty-five minutes.

46. Nevertheless, the signs of innovative preference are not entirely unmixed. In the earliest days of Alpha's existence, when the firm's financial position was precarious, the CEO was noticeably cautious and tried to minimize risk by deliberately emulating the strategy of his competitors until he achieved some financial security. This caution is probably explained by two points. First, even a fairly distinct innovative preference does not imply a complete lack of normal prudence. Second, in the early days of his business career, the CEO seems to have been very conscious of his own lack of business experience and management skills, which was probably a major factor in his decision to emulate successful peers until he gained confidence. He neither emulated, nor visibly exercised caution, after that time. Hence the overall picture that emerges is still one of a distinct innovative preference.

explained in Chapter 2, Eduard Spranger's theory says there are actually six possible motivations rather than three, so we must watch for instances where none of the three standard motivations (materialism, egotism or altruism) is dominant.

48. An altruist might also sometimes fix on a non-human class of beneficiaries, such as a natural ecology. This concept goes beyond Spranger's actual theory, which was first published in 1914, but seems to be a necessary extension in view of modern developments.

49. Interviewer: What made you decide "I have to do it myself"?

    CEO: Oh, I was working for a boss, and I was working twelve hours (a day)—seven 'til seven in the morning, and (when on the other shift) seven 'til seven at night, and I just thought well, if I'm putting all those hours in, why don't I try and start my own business?

    Interviewer: Because you'd make more money or because you'd have more freedom or because he wasn't doing it the way you wanted to do it and you needed to ...

    CEO: All of the above. I wanted a challenge. And I'd say challenge was the main thing I wanted—to prove to myself that I could do it. And I wanted to prove to the (doubters) that I would last (more than) three months.

50. CEO: You can go out and ask a guy out there (in the factory) now, who's come from the opposition who (went into liquidation), who's seen me make decisions immediately. And I've walked out of the room and he's said to my daughter, "Is he really going to go and do that?" And my daughter said "Yes."

51. Interviewer: But I want to get back to how long does it take to make a decision.

    CEO: Now, five minutes.

    Interviewer: Even a big decision?

    CEO: Half a million dollars decision can get made.

    Interviewer: And it's not done with filling in the columns (on a spreadsheet analysis)?

    CEO: No.

52. General Manager: (The CEO) spends quite a bit of time going out to companies, and (he) knows what's there, what parts they're making. He knows what the capacity in (their factory) building (is), and (what the capacities of) his own machines are. So he basically goes in there, and he goes to an exhibition (of metal-cutting machines), and two and two becomes four. I know that this customer's got this part (and is currently making it in-house). I know I can make it on this machine (shown at the exhibition); I can't do it

on the existing machine. Or if I do make it on the existing machine, I can't make it cheap enough. And of the quality they require.

Interviewer: Now there're lots and lots of repetition businesses that use a different philosophy of, if you keep (their factories) on a shoestring they'll be the low cost bidder. And so they run ratty old machines and tired old tools and do all that stuff. How do you weigh up that and how do you decide to be the guy at the up-market end of the spectrum as far as the plant and equipment's concerned?

CEO: I'd say just have balls.

53. It is worth noting however that where a matter was important enough, in the later years, he liked to have someone he trusted make a technical analysis to verify that his decision was affordable—but only after he was committed in his own mind:

CEO: ... when we're buying the machinery, we're talking half a million dollar machines—one go, one punch—we sit down and we do go through it and check it right out.

Interviewer: This is after you've already decided, but ...

CEO: Yes, I just want to confirm it, so I'm not going to wake up at two o'clock in the morning in a lather of sweat and have an ulcer.

54. Interviewer: What I'm trying to get hold of is what was the actual process for making these decisions. Does this go from...you've got one, (very low capability) lathe and this is OK, there's a living in this business, and if you go to some bigger scale there's a better living—what's the next step?

CEO: The next step has really been "I like new toys."

55. CEO: You just see something and go for it.

Interviewer: Why?

CEO: If you see something you want, you go and do it, don't you?

Interviewer: Is it because you want it, or because you think it's going to work?

CEO: Both.

56. CEO: I could easily say I'm not going to buy another thing, and sit back and put the money in the bank and have a world holiday. But that's not in me yet, because this vision is still to put another eight more machines out there. And win some really huge overseas contracts.

57. CEO: No, no, it happened very late. I think the single spindle (autolathes) down the back (of the factory) was (a case of) buying a machine that I knew I could get work for...that I knew I could survive. Once you survive and own a property and own a building and you've got money in the bank, then you

ng at the new technology. And the new technology has only come factory) in the last twelve years.

...er: OK, now how did that happen? Was it because it wasn't working well enough before? Or because you'd always wanted to do this but you couldn't afford to?

CEO: Because—I still go back to saying that when I went to Japan it opened my eyes very quickly.

58. CEO: But see with (the General Manager) if I can suggest (we do something), (the General Manager) will come in and say "No." Then we sit down and we have a good discussion about it, and we still say ...

General Manager: (Laughs).

59. Interviewer: So before you decided to buy the machine, you said OK, I'm going to buy a machine or whatever, or rent one, or—

CEO: No, I went and bought the machine first, then went and got the job.

Interviewer: OK, so you had your neck out a fair way then. Would you do that again?

CEO: I've been doing it every day but I've lived.

CEO: The classic fear has been that not having another director, and not having a partnership (has been a concern but) I've (seen) companies that have had three and four people—you can't run a business when two people want to take the money and run, and one wants to (continue to invest in expansion)—you can't do anything. So, it's my call, I live by my sword and (if necessary) I die by it. It's hanging up on the wall (points to Japanese ceremonial sword on wall). If I make a bad decision, it only comes back onto me.

3
A Clear, Coherent Strategy Concept

As explained in Chapter 1, the purpose of this book is to present a way to understand and analyze where organizations and individual people are headed, how they would get there, and why and how that course came to be adopted. The usual term for this direction-and-path concept is strategy, although other conceptions of strategy also exist in the professional literature.[60]

If real-world examples of a concept are to be understood, analyzed, and compared, the concept itself has to be able to support close scrutiny. We could not describe or compare the speeds of objects if we lacked a specific, clear, consistent way to measure and report speed. For similar reasons we cannot make a detailed analysis or comparison of individual strategies unless we use a specific, clear, consistent way of characterizing them. The required clarity does not exist in the mainstream strategy literature, which consists of a multitude of streams, interpretations, and theories that themselves are almost invariably outlined rather than specified. One of the essential steps toward meeting this book's objective is, therefore, to develop a suitable conception of strategy. The conception must be not only clear and meaningful—it must also help us to model and analyze, and it must be generally compatible with as much of the strategy literature as possible so that insights that have been explained previously are relevant and applicable.

POLICY, STRATEGY AND TACTICS

The military—the original source of the strategy concept[61]—is the only field where there are specific and fairly generally agreed upon definitions of policy, strategy, and tactics. Henry Mintzberg observed,[62] "In the military, policy deals with the purposes for which wars are fought, which is supposed to be the responsibility of the politicians. In other words, the politicians make policy, the generals, strategy."[63]

That is, the highest decision-domain concerns policy. Decisions are based there as to whether to fight a war, and if so, the underlying purpose of the war. The second level decision-domain relates to strategy, and is the home of decisions on *how* to achieve that underlying purpose. A specific group of people makes the decisions in each domain.

Descending one further level, in the fifth century BC, Sun Tzu emphasized the existence of separate strategic and tactical domains,[64] and in the nineteenth century, Clausewitz specifically defined the difference between them: strategy relates to "conduct of the war" while tactics relate to "conduct of the battle."[65] Usually the conduct of the war is a matter for the strategist—a collective term for certain upper-echelon generals and their staffs. The management of battles is delegated to tacticians—decentralized headquarters commanding specific theatres or battle-groups—subject to broad oversight from the strategist. Some tactical processes serve strategic purposes, but others do not. The extent to which strategically-irrelevant battles are avoided is one of the indicators of how efficiently the strategy is being implemented.

Tactical processes are enabled by operational processes. In theory, operational processes are always strategically irrelevant, and like strategically irrelevant battles, they need to be minimized to conserve resources for strategically relevant purposes.[66] Meanwhile the politicians, as policy makers, observe the entire conduct of the war and if necessary exercise veto power or replace personnel. While the politicians have the power to intervene in strategic or even tactical or operational decisions, they usually do not exercise this power extensively because they normally lack both expertise and deep situational understanding.

In the civilian context, the use of the terms policy, strategy, and tactics has not developed with equivalent clarity. Chester Barnard explained that the word policy had acquired such a diffuse and inconsistent range of meanings that he personally preferred to avoid it,[67] and the most influential of the foundational authors of the strategy literature, Kenneth Andrews, said that he chose to "sidestep the problem of drawing distinctions between objectives, policy, and programs of action."[68] However to satisfy the purpose of this book, clear domain-distinctions must be made, and I contend that the military terms can readily be applied to the civilian field. Just as government, using powers acquired from the general public, is responsible for all military action and directly determines military policy, organizations' boards are empowered by members or shareholders to ensure that the organizations are constructively directed and properly managed. This responsibility begins with what I propose to call policy—the board interprets and asserts the underlying purpose of the organization. Due to lack of time, expertise, and detailed knowledge, boards are likely to delegate the creation of strategy—the way the underlying purpose is pursued—to management.[69] A board usually communicates with management through a chief executive, who is thus empowered to determine strategy subject to approval by the board. Those employees deeply involved in strategic thinking and decision-making, which usually means or at least includes the chief executive, can collectively be called the organization's strategist. As in military strategy, civilian organizations' strategies consist of broad concepts that must be supported by specific tactics describing how they are to be executed. Only a truly fundamental description of how the entire organization addresses its underlying purpose is strategy; all else is tactical or operational. Usually not all tactical matters contribute directly to executing the strategy, and in theory, few if any operational matters do so.[70]

We can summarize the concept of domains set out in the preceding paragraphs as follows:

Proposition 1: Strategy operates in a bounded domain.

DEVELOPING SOME SPECIFIC CHARACTERISTICS

Strategy, like other social constructs,[71] is non-physical and does not have an objectively-verifiable nature. The meaning of the term, therefore, is determined by its users. If several different meanings exist, we can regard each as provisionally valid if it cannot be falsified—for example, by demonstrating internal logical flaws. Nevertheless, there are practical advantages in seeking to make each individual meaning of a construct as consistent as possible with others, so that theories developed and lessons learned in relation to one meaning will help to inform and guide users of other meanings. Earlier in the chapter, I pointed out that to satisfy the purposes of this book we need a conception of strategy that facilitates modeling and analysis. We can achieve this by insisting that strategy have a series of specific characteristics, which will be developed in this chapter. So long as these characteristics are compatible with each other and with the literature, we can accept them as a satisfactory solution. The conception of strategy that we adopt defines the boundaries of the strategic domain. We can do this quite arbitrarily, because declaring that something lies outside the strategic domain does not consign it to non-existence; it merely relegates it to the policy, tactical, or operational domain. I have devised a simple test for basic compatibility with the literature, and applied it in this chapter.[72]

Coherence and Focus

We can support our objective of making it possible to analyze and model strategy by insisting that any strategy has a single, coherent focus or theme. This is a major step toward distinguishing between strategy and tactics, and is legitimate for the purposes of this book if it is generally compatible with the literature—a requirement that seems to be satisfied.[73]

If a strategy appears to have more than one focus, four possibilities should be considered. The first is that we are not viewing the position at a high enough level; the true focus of a strategy will be obscured if we are insufficiently rigorous in excluding tactical matters. The second possibility is that the absence of focus is due to an absence of strategy; the entity may not have an overall theme or focus beyond the "react to events" level. Cyert and March (1963) supplied a detailed description of how and why this situation can arise. Such organizations may not be uncommon—indeed one is encountered in the analysis chapters of this book.[74] The third possibility is that the organization is strategically incoherent. The fourth possibility is that more than one strategy is in operation simultaneously—a situation that is seldom desirable and is usually arrived at inadvertently. This will be discussed near the end of the chapter.

Proposition 2: A strategy has a single, coherent focus.

Direction and Path

I indicated at the beginning of the chapter that I intended to adopt a direction-and-path concept of strategy. In other words, in this book a strategy consists of an overall goal, and an outline of a way to reach it. This concept seems to be generally compatible with the literature.[75]

Proposition 3: A strategy consists of a basic direction and a broad path.

Deconstruction

One of the implications of Proposition 3 is that any strategy can be expressed as multiple elements. If a strategy invariably consists of a basic direction *and* a broad path, at a minimum it must contain two elements. However while Proposition 2 requires that a strategy has a single focus, or basic direction, there is no corresponding requirement to express the broad path in just one element if it can be set out more clearly and in fewer words by subdividing it. This implies that deconstruction of a strategy into its elements can be approached as a reverse-synthesis process, working from a description of the strategy. The process consists firstly of capturing its basic direction, then secondly of stating the essential thrusts that cumulatively summarize the broad path for its execution.[76]

Proposition 4: A strategy can be deconstructed into elements.

Deconstructing Alpha's Basic Direction

Alpha was a start-up business at the beginning of the first phase of the case, and the founder was the sole owner—so he had to determine his underlying purpose before working out a strategy. He established his purpose by considering broad policy issues. First, he recognized that he was dissatisfied with his position as a tradesman in someone else's firm, due to powerlessness; his ambitions seemed unlikely to be realized,[77] and he disagreed with the prevailing business strategy.[78] Second, he considered alternative businesses he might go into, and chose metal-machining.[79] He then began thinking about strategy. Our first step in analyzing his strategy is to deconstruct it by identifying the basic direction and broad path for each of the two phases of the case.

First Phase

The newly established firm's basic direction was to launch a new business successfully, despite undercapitalization and lack of business skills or knowledge. The CEO-to-be intended to get started, and then achieve some momentum and stability, while simultaneously minimizing the risk (in the context, of course, of what was inherently a risky situation). In short, the basic direction was to *seek a low risk means to get into the business.*

Second Phase

What was the basic direction in the second phase? Obviously, the outcome was to achieve a market advantage by differentiating Alpha from its competitors. Alpha acquired a greater capability than others had, leading to advantages in flexibility, quality, and ability to satisfy customers' needs. The firm also developed an advantage in lead time,[80] and a lower variable cost per item produced on the more complex jobs.[81] Summarizing, Alpha's basic direction was *differentiation as capability leader* in its field.

Simplicity and Explicitness

To help us analyze strategy we can require that each of the essential thrusts must express a clear and distinct intent—but it must constitute a broad high-level statement of that intent, not a detailed plan. In deciding how to specify this as a requirement, we have the opportunity to make the analytical process as convenient and elegant as possible without conflicting with the foundational literature. Adopting two principles can help us achieve this. First, strategy should inherently be suited to simplicity of expression. Second, strategy should embrace the principle of conceptual parsimony. We can implement these principles by adding another Proposition to supplement Proposition 2 in creating a specific boundary between strategy and tactics. These two propositions together would then make the strategic domain quite small, and insist on its contents being highly coherent. The new Proposition would also result in the number of essential thrusts being small, expanding the tactical domain to contain all that is excluded by

Proposition 2 and the new Proposition from the strategic domain. The distinction between the two domains would then become clear and explicit. This intention can be implemented by the following Proposition:[82]

Proposition 5: Each of a strategy's essential thrusts is a single coherent concept directly addressing the delivery of the basic direction.

Deconstructing Alpha's Essential Thrusts

First Phase

Alpha's first-phase broad path was the way the firm sought to achieve its basic direction— *seek a low risk means to get into the business.* The path consisted of three essential thrusts. The first was *receiving encouragement* from potential customers while the CEO still worked for his last employer—thus, addressing what he saw as the greatest risk, the risk of not getting production contracts.[83] The second essential thrust was *emulation* of the strategic posture of the firm's competitors—minimizing costs by choosing well-worn, obsolescent machinery.[84] The third essential thrust was *rapid early growth* to speed Alpha through the vulnerable entry stage of being a sub-scale producer.[85] That third thrust was enabled by a tactical decision the CEO made: he would reinvest Alpha's earnings.[86] In brief, the broad path was simply a combination of the CEO verifying that he could get work, a clear intention to copy his competitors, and a determination to achieve quick growth.[87]

Second Phase

The second-phase broad path had to deliver the basic direction— *differentiation as capability leader.* It consisted of two essential thrusts. First, a pronounced *technology emphasis* was the source of Alpha's ability to produce more complex products than its competitors, and with less lead time. Second, Alpha focused on finding practical and affordable ways to give its customers *superior technical service.* These two essential thrusts were separate, complementary measures to address the same basic direction. In combination with the tactical enabler (reinvestment), either of them could have been used individually to achieve some measure of differentiation as capability leader.

Channel of Influence

A channel of influence is a linkage: a tendency for some force or action to bring about some type of outcome. If we ask a shopkeeper for an item on display, and pay the price, a conventional commercial channel of influence comes into play—the shopkeeper is aware of possible adverse social and economic consequences if the deal is not completed, so we will probably get what we asked and paid for. Applying the concept more broadly, an effective strategy must incorporate channels of influence; that is, it must inherently promote the desired outcome.[88] Without valid channels of influence, a grand plan for success is not a strategy; it is merely a collection of pious hopes. It is useful when forming or evaluating strategy, to find out *how* each proposed action is to achieve the intended result; that is, identify the channel of influence. A simple typology of channels of influence is, therefore, a basic tool for understanding strategy.

In Chapter 2 we divided any organization's environment into three parts (external, internal, and shareholder), and the ways the environment can be influenced into two types (rational and social). This potentially gives us six generic channels of influence: external rational, external social, internal rational, internal social, shareholder rational, and shareholder social. This typology appears consistent with some major themes of the professional literature.[89]

External Rational

The first of the six ways strategy can influence real-world outcomes—the external rational channel of influence—rests on the proposition that each organization is a free, flexible, rational operator in a world of rational external competitors and customers. Success is achieved by appealing to reason; that is, making a better offer than anyone else does, by out-playing competitors in an ongoing game. Because the game is rational, theoretical analysis and optimization are feasible.[90] Strategy, therefore, should be developed using economic tools including games theory and decision theory. Under this model, the market as a whole has power over its individual suppliers, rather than any one supplier having sustained power over the market.

External Social

The second of the six ways strategy can influence real-world outcomes—external social—asserts that an organization's success is partly determined by human behavior in the outside world. Nearly all important decisions are made by people, and people are not universally equipped with a perfect and rational understanding, or exclusively motivated by the pursuit of economic advantage. Instead, people's understanding is usually incomplete, and their motivations are more diverse and less rational. As well as being only partly rational, society is also only partly rule-bound, which sometimes invalidates the relevance of games theory. Strategy, therefore, can be made more successful if the organization analyzes and influences external audiences by applying various branches of psychology.[91]

Internal Rational

The third of the six ways strategy can influence real-world outcomes—internal rational—relies on the world being rational. Strategy, therefore, can be analyzed and optimized by applying economic concepts. The internal rational view differs from the external rational view by theorizing that, if the world were as free and responsive as the external rationalists claim, there would necessarily be a single optimum solution to every issue and the various rational competitors would, therefore, quickly find themselves all doing the same thing.[92] Observation of the real world, however, reveals substantial variations in individual organizations' levels of success. This implies that there are also internal factors in organizations that affect outcomes. If this is true, one path to superior performance involves capturing or creating a supply of these internal factors. Such factors typically consist of capabilities or resources within the organization that are attractive or even essential to customers, but are in short supply in the market for some reason—usually because they are difficult or impossible for competitors to replicate or imitate.[93] Therefore, one way an organization can become more successful than its competitors is by dominating the available supply of specific scarce resources such as brands, patents, skills and arts, raw materials, and product distribution channels. This resource advantage should give the firm market power.

Internal Social

The fourth of the six ways strategy can influence real-world outcomes—internal social—shares the external social way's view that social forces are important determinants of an organization's success; human beings do not act entirely rationally or pursue only economic goals, so understanding and influencing people requires the use of psychology. However, like the internal rational view, it concludes that some of the performance limitations and enabling factors arise inside the organization rather than outside it. Many studies and analyses have shown that getting everyone in an organization vigorously following the same plan or even the same objectives, can be extremely difficult—especially if you want them to be the particular plan and objectives chosen by top management.[94] One of the aims of strategy, therefore, should be influencing and aligning the organization's own processes and personnel. This view of strategy includes several streams of literature.[95]

Shareholder Rational and Shareholder Social

As explained in Chapter 2, the purpose of strategy is aligning the outcome with the organization's underlying purpose. This implies that adjusting the latter is just as useful as changing the former. The underlying purpose is the means by which those theoretically in command of the organization—such as its shareholders, external members, or the electors of its leaders—control what is actually done. Normally, there are sanctions these groups can apply if they are dissatisfied; for example, they can replace members of the board of directors, withhold funds, or switch their membership and support to rival organizations. Consequently, defying the key external group is often unwise, but when managers are making allocation decisions, they have other priorities that compete with the shareholders' desires. There may be business opportunities outside the limits dictated by the current underlying purpose,[96] and employees may prefer to consume resources that the underlying purpose would direct toward performance-enhancement.[97] Hence, strategists use various techniques to influence the shareholder group and, thus, modify the underlying purpose. The respective arguments for using either rational or social influence-techniques for this are the same ones explained previously for external rational and external social channels of influence.[98]

Paradigmatic Views

Well-known literature based on empirical research contains examples of most of the six channels of influence.[99] Because strategists have cognitive biases, when they choose channels of influence for their strategies they rely on their personal conceptions of how the world functions. We have found six generic channels of influence, but for some strategists just one of these may be so firmly entrenched as to make the other explanations seem implausible or irrelevant. Other strategists may have access to more than one of the channels, but nevertheless display a preference.

An entrenched way of thinking that limits or prevents its adherents' access to other ways is often called a paradigm.[100] When analyzing real cases we should always watch for indications of whether the strategists' choices are influenced by paradigmatic views.

Practical Implications of Channels of Influence

To be valid, a strategy must imply how it is to take effect in the real world; that is, it must be associated with specific channels of influence. Proposition 3 divides any strategy into two sections. First, the basic direction is centrally concerned with *goals*, outlining the high level outcome of the strategy with little or no reference to how it might be achieved. Second, the broad path answers a *means* question, outlining the way this outcome is to be brought about.[101] Proposition 5 requires that each element of the broad path—each essential thrust—must directly address the delivery of the basic direction. However, this alone is not sufficient to ensure that a thrust can contribute to achieving the basic direction; it must also be capable of having an effect. To have an effect the thrust must imply a channel of influence. An allegedly-essential thrust that has no channel of influence is merely a pious hope.

Proposition 6: A strategy's essential thrusts each imply a specific channel of influence.

Classifying Alpha's Channels of Influence

We classify strategy content according to which of the six generic channels of influence each essential thrust relied on most: external rational, internal rational, external social, internal social, shareholder rational, or shareholder social.

First Phase

Alpha's first-phase strategy must have been based on some causal relationship; the basic direction was to minimize risk, and there must have been some mechanism for achieving this. We infer these causal relationships by looking at the individual essential thrusts. The basic direction says what will be done, and the broad path says how it will be done; only the latter requires a channel of influence. The aim of the first essential thrust, *receiving encouragement*, was to ensure that Alpha would have initial customers, by taking advantage of the founder's pre-existing personal relationships with some of them. This is an example of an external social channel of influence.[102] The concept of the second thrust, *emulation*, was to create a temporary implicit cartel with Alpha's competitors. As long as all competitors had the same (rather inadequate) production equipment, customers had no real alternative to accepting it. This is an example of an external rational channel.[103] The third thrust, *rapid early growth*, was aimed at minimizing the time for which Alpha was vulnerable due to its initial lack of size and resources. It is an example of an internal rational channel.[104] In summary, the first thrust's channel of influence was external social, the second thrust's was external rational, and the third thrust's was internal rational.

Second Phase

The second phase began when the CEO abandoned his initial defensive strategy and became aggressive. The new basic direction was *differentiation as capability leader* and it was to be achieved through *technology emphasis* and *superior technical service*. Again, we must infer the causal relationship: how would this strategy make Alpha successful? The CEO's descriptions of how and why he made decisions in the second phase tended to be focused on gaining an advantage over competitors by making a superior rational offer to customers.[105] Both of the essential thrusts—*technology emphasis* and *superior technical service*—were aimed at winning by delivering specific, rational customer benefits that competitors were not prepared to match. Alpha did not have market power; it took advantage of its competitors' conservatism.[106] Both of the essential thrusts, therefore, can be classed as *external rational*.

Deliberate or Emergent

The best-known early strategy literature was only concerned with deliberate strategy formation—creating strategy by strategic thinking and decision-making.[107] Soon afterward, a new branch of literature was introduced,[108] based on the concept of emergent strategy formation: strategy emerging implicitly from a stream of tactical and operating decisions without any involvement of strategic thinking and decision-making. This literature stream pointed out that sometimes what is intended by a strategist can metamorphose during the transition into realized strategy—intended content can be edited, and emergent content can be added, in the course of a series of tactical or operational decisions.[109] Nevertheless, because of Proposition 5, while a strategy can include essential thrusts formed both deliberately and emergently, these two types of process are mutually-exclusive at the level of individual thrusts.[110]

Nothing in Propositions 1 to 6 excludes the possibility of a strategy being entirely emergent. Such an outcome would merely require that there was no involvement of the strategic domain, and no transition from intended strategy to realized strategy. The entire strategy, including the basic direction, would then simply emerge as a pattern in various tactical and operational decisions—a process called "purely retroactive" strategy formation.[111] Whether it is an entire purely retroactive strategy or just individual essential thrusts of a strategy with a deliberate basic direction, emergent strategy can only be identified and described after retrospective synthesis based on the entity's entire behavior.[112] The outcome of this examination is typically a description of the implemented strategy whether it was formed deliberately, emergently, or by a combination of the two, but under the reasoning we have developed in this chapter it can also be expressed as a specific set of indivisible elements, each of which must have been formed either deliberately or emergently.

Deliberate strategy formation is centered on strategic thinking: cognition and conscious decisions in the strategic domain. Strategic thinking necessarily involves willingness to reconsider both the entity's basic direction, and all of its broadest action-intentions to implement that direction (that is, the essential thrusts). Subsequent activities associated with winning support for the strategy and implementing it are parts of the transition from intended strategy to realized strategy; strategic thinking is only involved in this transition if the strategist consciously re-opens the content of the strategy for further review.

When the final elements of a strategy have been identified, the distinction between those formed deliberately and emergently is based on fact—which of them were adopted in discrete conscious strategic decisions, and which were implicit products of a number of lesser decisions? The difference between a strategic decision (the only kind taken in the strategic domain) and a non-strategic decision (taken in the tactical domain, or perhaps in the even-lower operational domain) is whether those taking it deliberately undertook strategic thinking and then deliberately embraced the creation of an element of strategy.

There is a requirement that follows logically from the preceding reasoning: a strategy with an emergent basic direction must necessarily be purely retroactive. It cannot contain deliberate essential thrusts, since it is impossible to make strategic decisions to adopt such thrusts without having already made a strategic decision to adopt the basic direction they are intended to support. It is, of course, possible to make a strategic decision to adopt a basic direction that already existed as part of a purely retroactive strategy, but that decision transforms the basic direction from emergent to deliberate. Deliberate strategy is formed in the strategic domain, and implemented in the tactical domain. Emergent strategy formation and implementation occur simultaneously, in the tactical domain, with no involvement of the strategic domain.

Proposition 7: A strategy's constituent elements are each formed either deliberately or emergently.

Before classifying how each element of Alpha's strategy was formed, I will introduce a universal model explaining strategy process. I will apply the model when classifying Alpha's strategy components.

A FRAMEWORK MODEL OF STRATEGY FORMATION

Propositions 1 to 7 give strategy specific properties, and imply a clear model of how strategy forms. The model is shown in Figure 1.[113] In explaining the model, I will refer to processes by their locations in this figure.

FIGURE 1: SIMPLE MODEL OF STRATEGY FORMATION

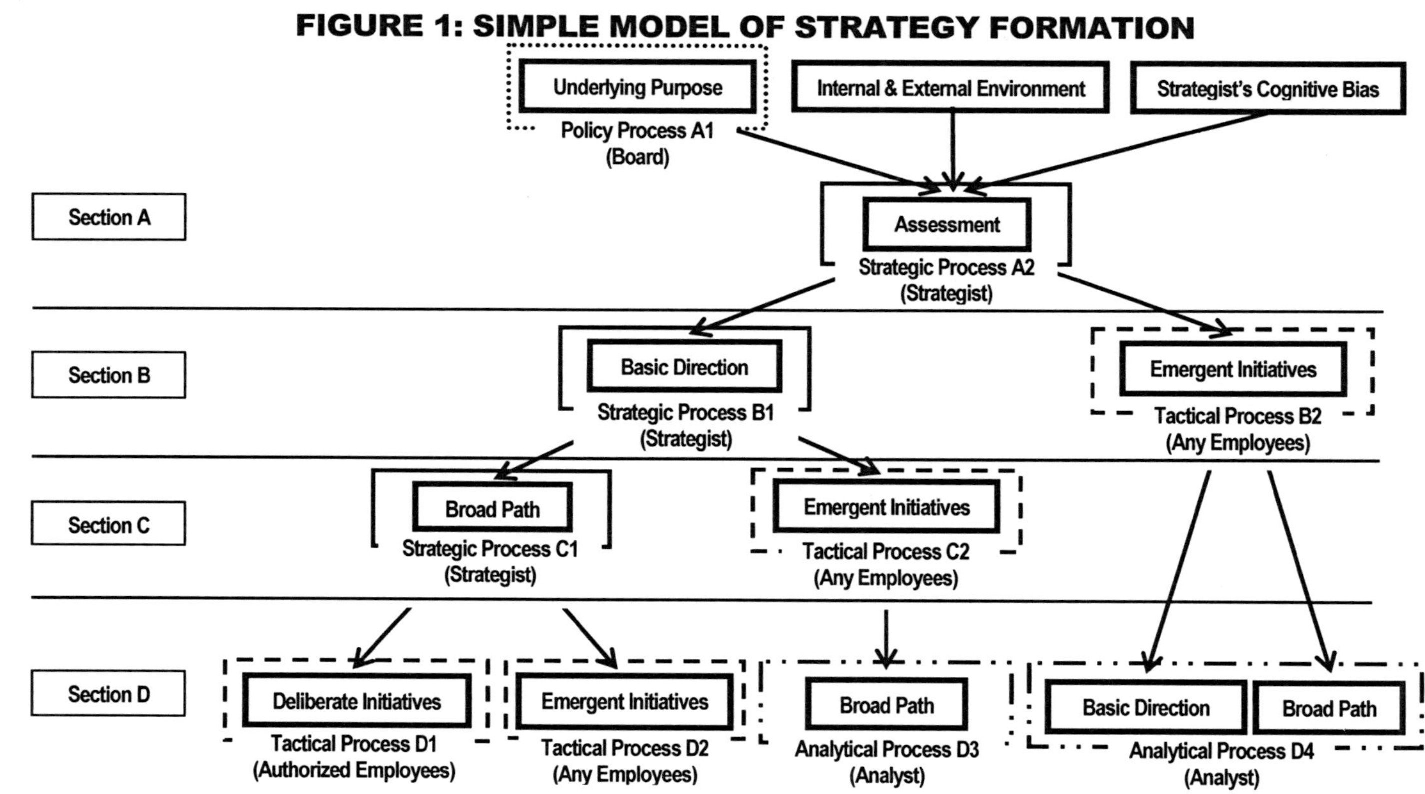

Strategy formation begins with the three sets of circumstances that guide and constrain strategic choices (A).[114] The first is the underlying purpose of the organization, which is usually interpreted and enforced by the board (A1).[115] The second is the internal and external environment; that is, the strategic context inside and outside the organization itself. The third is the strategist's personal cognitive bias: a distorting lens through which the world is viewed. Cognitive bias explains why different strategists choose different solutions to the same strategic problems.[116] Based on these three factors, the strategist makes an assessment and decides whether to engage in deliberate strategy formation (A2).

Whether the strategist engages in deliberate strategy formation or not, a basic direction is likely to be created (B):[117] the decision from Process A2 only determines whether deliberate or emergent process is used. Using deliberate process (B1) implies consciously choosing an overall strategic theme or objective, which we call a basic direction. If the strategist does not engage in a deliberate strategy formation process, no conscious strategic thinking or strategic decisions occur, implying that he or she is open-minded, or inert or ineffectual, but over time, various tactical and operational decisions made in the organization will have strategic implications. When the key decisions are identified after the event and interpreted as a coherent series of actions, they can be viewed as what I will call emergent initiatives. I will return to this point when describing the last section of the model (D).[118]

If a basic direction has been produced deliberately,[119] the next section of the model (C) offers the same two ways to take the next step: deliberate or emergent process. The outcome of deliberate process (C1)[120]—or strategic thinking—will be the deliberate adoption of one or more broad path elements, which we call essential thrusts. If emergent process is followed (C2), there will be no strategic thinking, but eventually emergent initiatives will be created by actions that have unintended strategic implications, in a similar way to what would have happened in the previous section of the model if emergent process had occurred (B2).[121]

The final section of the model (D) shows how strategy can be implemented. We can begin by considering how any essential thrusts that were adopted deliberately (C1) are to take effect in the tactical domain.[122] Essential thrusts are broad, high-level concepts and transforming them into specific, executable programs requires tactical action-initiatives. The required initiatives can be produced in either or both of two ways. The first alternative consists of addressing one or more of the deliberate essential thrusts and consciously creating deliberate tactical initiatives to implement them (D1).[123] The second alternative operates differently; it does not require thinking about the essential thrusts or taking deliberate action to implement them (D2).[124] Instead, emergent initiatives simply develop in the course of business, as various practical actions either support or reshape the essential thrusts by supplementing or subverting any initiatives that arise from the first alternative (D1).[125] All initiatives, whether deliberate or emergent, are created by tactical and operational processes; they do not involve strategic thinking. Now, having looked at how deliberate essential thrusts (from C1) can be implemented, we can turn to the process for implementing emergent essential thrusts (from C2).[126] This is the third process shown in the final section of the model (D3). Emergent thrusts inherently consist of a series of practical initiatives, and by using process D3 an analyst could synthesize these initiatives retrospectively into emergent essential thrusts.[127] The strategy's full broad path includes every essential thrust supporting the basic direction, whether produced deliberately or emergently. However, under Proposition 7, each essential thrust must result from one or another of these, not both.[128]

The previous paragraph describes how strategy forms if the strategist engages in strategic thinking and adopts a deliberate basic direction (B1).[129] However, I have also referred to an alternative approach: if the strategist does not engage in strategic thinking, emergent initiatives will probably develop anyway (B2).[130] Eventually, an analyst could review all of the initiatives from Process B2 as a set, and identify the purely retroactive emergent strategy implicit in them (D4).[131] Like strategy formed deliberately, strategy formed by a purely retroactive emergent process must consist of a basic direction and a broad path in that direction. Indeed, there is no difference at a content level between deliberate strategy and emergent strategy; the only difference is in the formation and implementation processes. Strategy can be formed deliberately by a strategist, or emergently as the aggregate of contributions from everyone who makes a decision that turns out to have strategic implications.

Classifying Alpha's Strategy Process

First Phase

The model shows that the first step in strategy formation must be either deliberate (B1) or emergent (B2). Process B1 is characterized by the strategist engaging in strategic thinking, and consciously adopting a basic direction. In Process B2 however, the strategist is "open-minded or inert or ineffectual" and does not engage in true strategic thinking. The first question, then, is whether the Alpha CEO consciously chose a first-phase basic direction for the firm. It is evident that he did, so the strategy was deliberate (B1).[132]

Continuing in Figure 1, after forming a deliberate basic direction, the next step must have been formation of a broad path. Each essential thrust of that path must have been formed either deliberately (C1) or emergently (C2), depending on whether strategic thinking was involved. The CEO consciously recognized the first essential thrust, *receiving encouragement*, as a necessary precursor to going into business. While he seemed to indicate that he did nothing to prompt his potential customers to give him this encouragement,[133] he recognized its importance and consciously included it in his completed strategy. This means that the first essential thrust was deliberate strategy (C1). The CEO emphasized his awareness of an initial lack of financial capacity, and that this led him to follow his competitors' approach,[134] so the second essential thrust, *emulation,* was deliberate strategy (C1). The CEO included the third essential thrust, *rapid early growth,* because until the business reached critical mass, he could not feel secure enough to begin to exercise power and make the choices he wanted to make.[135] Therefore, it was a result of strategic thinking and was deliberate strategy (C1). To summarize, all components of the first phase strategy were deliberate, not emergent.

Second Phase

As in the first phase, the process model tells us that either a second-phase basic direction was formed deliberately (B1), or it arose emergently by default (B2). The CEO's original decision to buy one computer numerically controlled machining center began a process that would eventually differentiate Alpha as *capability leader* and make this the basic direction. That decision triggered the beginning of the second phase. However, there was no actual review of strategy, and Alpha went into the second phase with much of its first-phase strategy still in place. It bought one high-technology machine as a tactical initiative, without any specific intention of buying more. As it turned out, the first high-technology machine was so successful that the CEO bought more of them, and a pattern of behavior formed; an emphasis on these machines gradually became part of Alpha's strategy. Independently of this, the CEO made other individual decisions that, over time, cumulatively provided superior customer service. Thus, the basic direction (*capability leader*) did not exist prior to the broad path being put into effect; both basic direction and broad path were parts of a strategic package born of a series of tactical decisions over a period of years. This is a description of Process B2, not Process B1, so the entire second phase strategy was emergent. This was an instance of purely retroactive strategy formation.

Summary of the Alpha Case

Alpha was an example of a firm where an entrepreneurial CEO dominated every aspect of the business; indeed in many respects he designed the firm to be an expression of his personality. His decision criteria were consistently rational and often insightful, but his decision process was powerful and impulsive. He was capable of strategic thinking when it was strictly necessary, and he did this to establish a deliberate strategy before starting the business. Subsequently, however, he felt free to follow his preferences, and all of his thinking appears to have been tactical. This extensive tactical thinking ultimately produced a very coherent emergent strategy, but the coherence was probably achieved simply because one rather clear-thinking person was making all of the tactical decisions without consultation.

It is unusual to find a case as uncomplicated as Alpha's. It involved an experienced tradesman deciding to go into business for himself. After a few years, he felt confident in managing the business, which by then had a sound financial basis. From that time forward, he increasingly gave free rein to his inclinations. As it happened, his inclinations were highly ego-driven and this was reflected in many aspects of his business methods and practices, including the strategy content that could eventually be seen in the pattern of his tactical and operating decisions.

Most real-world strategy formation is heavily influenced by the organization's environment. Strategists are usually constrained within the organization by seemingly inviolable paradigms and by interest groups. Their choices are affected by external pressures—from members or shareholders, markets, boards of directors, government policies, regulatory agencies, and a multitude of other external forces—and by issues arising within the organization. They are also driven by cognitive bias, which strategists impose on the strategy formation task as an additional requirement. These various forces do not change the nature of the strategy-formation task, but they increase its complexity since each force has to be addressed, and because doing so can shape strategy.[136]

It is evident that the Alpha CEO thoroughly enjoyed running his company. Within wide limits, he was able to do pretty much as he wished, and he took advantage of this freedom. Few strategists are in that situation, as the other nine cases in this book will show. A strategist's task begins with mapping the feasible solution zone: the range of strategies that seem likely to achieve the underlying purpose reasonably efficiently. Freedom of action only exists within this zone. For the Alpha CEO, that zone was quite extensive. In the next few cases, however, we will see the walls gradually close in on the strategists.

APPLYING THE MODEL GENERALLY

Kenneth Andrews' description of strategy formation was based entirely on strategic thinking, and conscious implementation of the resulting deliberate strategy.[137] Where implementation is concerned, I suggest that this model was superficial, because it relied almost entirely on Tactical Process D1. Andrews only visualized a top-down command- and incentive-driven approach, saying, "A system of constraints, controls, and penalties must be devised to contain nonfunctional activity and to enforce standards."[138]

In practice, this type of top-down implementation of deliberate strategy is often difficult because it is likely to be resisted or subverted by the organization.[139] The overall result is that realized strategy sometimes differs in detail from intended strategy.[140] Andrews' prescription, even with the addition of informally-produced tactical initiatives supplementing the official ones (D2), does not explain all real-world strategy formation. Informal initiatives are not limited to changing strategy in detail; they can also add entire essential thrusts to what the strategist had intended and planned (C2).[141] This could happen two alternative ways, based on the motives of the operating managers who cause the emergent strategy to form. In the first version, individual managers aiming to maximize business performance automatically fill gaps in the official, deliberate strategy by taking action at a tactical or operating level. Repetition of these actions eventually establishes a coherent pattern that can be recognized as an additional essential thrust.[142] The second version of the process springs from more personal motives, such as particular sectional interests or dissent from senior management's intentions if they conflict with the organization's cultural values. An open-minded strategist might be aware of emergent essential thrusts formed by both process-versions. Those caused by conscientious managers finding ways to improve the business would be regarded as valuable supplements to the deliberate strategy. Those arising from personal or cultural factors might be tolerated as unavoidable outcomes of the organization's social nature.[143]

I have explained that informal processes can modify deliberate strategy, either at a detail level or by adding essential thrusts. However, these processes can go even further, and create an entire strategy without using strategic thinking at any stage, through what is called purely retroactive strategy formation (B2 and D4). This can happen in two ways, paralleling the two ways essential thrusts can be created informally through Process C2. In the first approach, the organization does not adopt any deliberate strategy, but managers and groups of managers routinely make operating or tactical decisions in pursuit of optimum business performance. After various evolutionary stages, a workable set of practices emerges as a functional strategy. The second approach is based on the concept that given the opportunity, people often pursue cultural, personal, or sectional agendas. Sometimes processes form around these agendas, eventually resulting in emergent strategies.[144]

The role of the strategist in purely retroactive strategy formation is an important issue. The model indicates that the formation of a complete strategy without any strategic thinking can only occur if the strategist is open-minded, or inert or ineffectual. One explanation of the open-minded strategist's role was offered by Ed Wrapp,[145] who described a pragmatic strategist concerned with achieving results without jeopardizing personal credibility by taking a visible position. He indicated that such strategists are ready to accept solutions from any quarter, while concealing their own agendas if they have them.[146] Similarly, a version of the inert or ineffectual strategist was modeled by Richard Cyert and James March.[147] In this operating mode, the organization proceeds without a deliberate strategy by reacting to situations as they arise. However as Mintzberg noted,[148] "Strategies grow like weeds in a garden." In other words, Cyert and March's strategy-free zone may sometimes be unstable; if the strategist does not act deliberately, the organization may fill the strategic vacuum emergently.

MULTIPLE STRATEGIES

The model leaves open the possibility of a firm having more than one strategy simultaneously—the test for multiple strategies being the existence of multiple basic directions. Multiple basic directions could arise in two ways. The first possibility stems from the model's definition of a strategist: a person, people, or group engaging or empowered to engage in strategic thinking and decision-making. It follows that there can be more than one deliberate strategy in place simultaneously if there is more than one strategist. The second possibility is that one or more purely retroactive strategies could develop, whether or not deliberate strategy existed as well.

Multiple deliberate strategies might form if an influential group saw the appointed strategist's offering as inadequate or inappropriate. The dissident group might then produce its own strategy, which might be either complementary to or competitive with the initial strategy. The implemented outcome or realized strategy would then be the result of social processes within the organization.[149] There might also be more than one dissident group; each competing group could try to maximize the extent to which its own agenda became part of the realized strategy. Bower and Gilbert have described individual groups seeking to inject tactical initiatives or even entire essential thrusts into their firms' strategies.[150] Conceivably such groups could be still more ambitious and pursue complete strategies including distinct basic directions. All sources engaging in strategic thinking and decision-making are strategists, so each can form a deliberate strategy. The realized outcome could, therefore, reflect a mixture of several deliberate strategies.

Emergent strategy forms as the unanticipated outcome of a series of decisions not intended to have strategic implications.[151] As explained above, it can consist merely of one or more emergent thrusts in support of a deliberate basic direction, or it can be a complete purely retroactive strategy. There seems to be no reason why all the emergent strategy formed must necessarily relate to a single basic direction, especially in large or compartmentalized organizations. Various emergent essential thrusts, therefore, might address several deliberate strategies, simultaneously with multiple purely retroactive emergent strategies.

Obviously, the analytical task of separating and deconstructing multiple strategies may be challenging. Indeed, some companies may be strategically incoherent, not because they have no strategy, but because they have several and lack the ability to reconcile them into one.

THE ANALYSIS

Analyzing strategy is like writing a book on history; a technical analysis of the raw data is required before an adequate narrative can be written. The analysis must be based on a combination of verifiable facts, and the statements of the people who actually made the decisions. It must be examined in detail, looking for gaps, conflicts, and incompatibility with the underlying conceptual framework. When it has passed this test, it can be used as the master-plot for the history—or in our case, for writing the narrative description of the strategy. I emphasize that neither the historian nor the strategy analyst creates the plot; they infer it from the actual words of the key players in the case. To be useful, a strategy analysis document must conform not only to what the players have said, but also to the precise meaning of the strategy construct as set out in Chapter 2 and this chapter.

The next section of the book continues the analysis of real cases, using this approach.[152]

NOTES

60. The two books that were strategy literature's main foundation – Andrews (1971) and Chandler (1962) – tolerated unspecified boundaries and incompletely-defined characteristics. The scope of the literature has tended to widen even further since then. Note that Andrews (1971) will be cited when referring to text that also appeared in Learned et al. (1965).

61. The term "strategy" arises from the Greek "strategos," which originally meant "the art of the (military) general officer."

62. (Mintzberg 1987a).

63. Kenneth Andrews made a similar point: "For the military, strategy is most simply the science and art of employing a nation's armed strength to secure goals prescribed by the nation's leaders" (1971 p. 27).

64. "All men can see these tactics whereby I conquer, but what none can see is the strategy out of which victory is evolved" (Sun 1944 p. 62).

65. "According to our classification, therefore, tactics is the theory of the use of military forces in combat. Strategy is the theory of the use of combats for the object of the war" (Clausewitz 1968 p. 173). Note that Clausewitz excludes determining the object of the war from his definition of strategy, thus implying the existence of a separate policy domain.

66. The distinction between strategically relevant and irrelevant processes rests on whether a particular process delivers a change in circumstances that materially advances the execution of the strategy. In the military, operational processes such as providing the armed forces with food, shelter, ammunition, equipment, coordination, organization, recruitment, training, discipline, morale, public relations, and various other services are clearly necessary to enable successful battles to take place, but normally they are not strategically relevant. However, see the section in this chapter comparing deliberate and emergent strategy formation; sometimes the final strategy is influenced by processes intended to be strategically irrelevant.

67. (Barnard 1940).

68. (Andrews 1971 p. 28).

69. (Andrews 1980).

70. It is desirable to give priority to strategic purposes when allocating resources, since this enables the organization to implement more of its strategy with the limited resources it has or can obtain. Note, however, that nominally nonstrategic processes sometimes influence both strategy formation and implementation. This will be discussed later in the chapter.

71. A construct is a concept that is considered by users to have a particular meaning, but is not directly observable. Examples from physical science include power and energy, while those from social science include personality and emotion.

72. To estimate influence on the literature, in March 2007 I searched the number of times various definitions were quoted (not cited) in the EBSCO Business Source Premier commercial database. Ten books and articles known to contain definitions of strategy (Chandler 1962 p. 13; Ansoff 1965 p. 94; Andrews

1971 p. 28; Vancil 1976; Mintzberg 1977; Hofer and Schendel 1978 pp. 23-24; Rumelt 1979 p. 179; Quinn 1980 p. 7; Miller and Toulouse 1998; Bower and Gilbert 2007) were tested individually. Two partial or near-definitions were also tested (Mintzberg 1994; Porter 1996). After excluding articles written by the author of each definition, the outcome of the searches was that Mintzberg's (1977) definition was quoted thirty-five times, Chandler's (1962 p. 13) twenty-three times, Quinn's (1980 p. 7) six times, and Andrews' (1971 p. 28) five times. None of the other definitions or near-definitions tested had been quoted repeatedly in subsequent literature. While it is inevitable that many more than ten definitions and two near-definitions exist, I suggest that frequently-quoted definitions are well-known and are, thus, relatively unlikely to have been missed. In the most-quoted definition, Henry Mintzberg (1977) said, "I propose to define strategy in general (and realized strategy in particular) as a pattern in a stream of decisions." Alfred Chandler (1962 p. 13) said, "Strategy can be defined as the determination of the basic long-term goals and objectives of an enterprise, and the adoption of courses of action and the allocation of resources necessary for carrying out these goals." James Brian Quinn's (1980 p. 7) definition was, "A strategy is the pattern or plan that integrates an organization's major goals, policies and action sequences into a cohesive whole." Kenneth Andrews (1971 p. 28) wrote, "For us corporate strategy is the pattern of major objectives, purposes, or goals and essential policies and plans for achieving those goals, stated in such a way as to define what business the company is in or is to be in and the kind of company it is or is to be."

73. Quinn's and Andrews' definitions referred to strategy as a single "pattern" with multiple "goals". Mintzberg's definition was also centered on strategy consisting of a single pattern. Chandler's definition, the first to be written, did not use the word pattern but may perhaps have hinted at a similar point. It said that strategy contains "the determination" (singular, not plural) of all of the most important goals and objectives. Thus, all of the definitions seem to be generally compatible with the concept that a strategy has a single, coherent focus; that is, they can all accommodate that requirement even if they do not demand it. In practical terms, the concept of coherence and focus implies that a strategy is to be approached as a unitary concept.

74. See Chapter 10. Lambda had this type of strategy in the second phase of the case.

75. Referring again to the four influential definitions of strategy, Mintzberg's definition was not specific about the content of the construct and, therefore, does not conflict with the direction-and-path concept. The other three definitions were somewhat more specific, and they all seem compatible with the view that strategy consists of an encompassing objective and a way to accomplish it; that is, a direction and a path.

None of the definitions expressed a clear boundary between strategy and tactics, but all except Mintzberg gave a general indication: Chandler used the word "basic," and Quinn and Andrews the word "major," to indicate that strategy is inherently confined to a high conceptual level. Those three authors' conceptions of strategy, therefore, set action-intentions, or the path, broadly not precisely, leaving specific intentions as tactical matters.

76. Quinn (1980 p. 80) introduced the term "essential thrusts." He asserted that it is impractical to pursue a large number of "strategic goals" simultaneously, so just a very few of the most important should be pressed at any one time. He referred to these selected goals as essential thrusts. I use the term essential thrust slightly differently, applying it to every element in the broad path, but making the strategy construct itself compact and manageable by restricting it to a very high conceptual level. I have done this by developing and applying Propositions 2 and 5.

77. CEO: I couldn't see a future there for me. There were four people above me, and they wouldn't know how to work (regardless of circumstances). They were useless. I could see that. And I thought I'm not going to wait for them to die.

78. CEO: Even if I was managing director there, if someone above me is saying you can't go and buy that machine, because we want to put the money in a holiday house, then there's no future in that business.

79. CEO: So it was a pastry cook, dental mechanic, or engineering, and engineering was going to win out, because I'd already put fifteen (or more) years into it.

80. Lead time is the time between deciding to introduce a product and having production quantities of the product available.

81. Variable cost is the incremental cost of making one more widget, once we have already set up the resources and facilities to make widgets. Hence it essentially consists of raw material cost, cost of machine operator's time, and actual wear-and-tear on the machinery and tooling to make one widget. It excludes fixed costs, which were described in a Note to Chapter 1. The sum of fixed costs and variable costs is the total cost of production.

    The following interview excerpt explains why the CEO chose the strategy he did.

    Interviewer: How is the part being made at the moment? By some dreadful manual technique?

    CEO: Yes. Probably three operations, three people doing three different things.

    Interviewer: You take it off the lathe, put it on the mill, all this kind of thing?

General Manager: Yes.

CEO: Repeatability's not there, operator doesn't turn up, backlog. This machine runs it around the clock.

Interviewer: OK. So the work wasn't being offered to repetition engineers because they didn't have the capability to do it, it was being done in other weird ways using semi-toolroom methods. And you knew you could make it into a regular repetition job if you had higher tech equipment.

CEO: Easy, yes.

Interviewer: So you did that, and you started in a small way, and found that this worked, your guess was right, you could get more work, and this was good business to have, because your only competitors were guys who were doing cottage-industry stuff.

CEO: Exactly right.

82. Richard Rumelt (1979 p. 197) once commented, "It is a frequent observation that one person's strategy is another's tactics – that what is strategic depends upon where you sit." This view is inconsistent with the concept of strategy implied by Propositions 1 through 5. The strategist looks at the situation in a specific division or functional group of the organization, and sees an individual battle. However, the executives in that division may lack the perspective to recognize that what they are engaged in is just part of the implementation of one of the strategy's essential thrusts. This may lead them to think—erroneously—that their tactical plans and decisions are strategic.

83. CEO: Well, there were a lot of people that had dealt with me for six years. And (they) said, "Why aren't you doing it yourself? We'll support you."

84. Interviewer: Using effectively the same as everybody else, that is, well, we'll use whatever machine is most affordable, and we'll make products that at least the customer doesn't send back, and that's the way the whole of Australia's automotive industry existed through the fifties and sixties at least?

    CEO: Yes.

    Interviewer: Now, you start off there, because that's all you can afford to do.

85. The following is an excerpt from the case study report:

    After five years, (Alpha) was a viable but very small business, consisting of the CEO (assisted by his wife) operating four second-hand autolathes, and having an opportunity to grow the business if he chose.

86. General Manager: One of the other conscious decisions (the CEO) has made is actually to reinvest in new machinery. A lot of people don't reinvest the profits of the company.

(The reinvestment decision was tactical rather than strategic because it did not directly address the strategy's basic direction. See Proposition 5.)

87. Of course, in the very early days his initial lack of economies of scale was also offset by extreme penny-pinching, but this was for a short time and can be viewed as tactical rather than strategic.

    (Economies of scale can be regarded as an improved ability to absorb fixed costs. That is, the firm's total revenue from all that it produces must recoup the total of its fixed and variable costs. Since (within limits) fixed costs do not increase with higher production, it is easier to recoup fixed costs if we have greater revenue, which is generated by higher sales.)

88. The term "channel of influence" always refers to a mechanism for causing a change, not a target for change.

89. The external rational view is the main topic of Porter (1980; 1985). Porter treated the organization's external environment as a field of competition in which each organization adjusts its structure, resources, and practices as often as necessary to create and hold a competitive advantage. The internal rational view is explained by Wernerfelt (1984). Wernerfelt pointed out that economic theory suggests successful externally-focused strategies will be replicated by competitors, so firms only obtain sustainable advantage through strategies that are not replicable. These are necessarily based on unique internal resources. An example of the external social view is given in Kohli and Jaworski (1990). They developed a "Market Orientation" construct and asserted that when analyzing opportunities, best results could be achieved by relying on a full understanding of the actual market context, instead of assuming that rational behavior and the tenets of pure economics would apply. Another aspect of external social influence was described by Hillman and Hitt (1999). They offered a "Public Policy" construct, asserting that government policies and decisions have a significant effect on external outcomes. Influencing these policies and responding effectively to them were, therefore, said to be powerful ways to improve organizations' effectiveness. An example of internal social influence is provided by Simon (1957). Simon said, "Administrative theory is peculiarly the theory of intended and bounded rationality – of the behavior of human beings who satisfice because they have not the wits to maximize" (1957 p. xxiv). A second example of an internal social channel was set out by Bower and Doz (1979). They asserted that "managers of today's multinationals are not so much economic decision makers as they are governors of a social and political strategic management process"(1979 p. 165). In an example of influence techniques being applied to the organization's shareholders, Pfeffer and Salancik (1978) treated each aspect of the environment, including the shareholders, as both sources of, and targets for, influence.

90. This external rational view of how strategy works was expounded broadly by Adam Smith in 1776 (Smith 1991) as an "invisible hand" that acts ruthlessly and relentlessly to guide most participants' behavior toward the most efficient option, despite the intentions of all of the individual strategists to gain special advantages for themselves. Whenever an individual finds a better way, it is quickly emulated and this results in a general improvement in economic performance (1991 p. 351). The corresponding rationale of how competitors analyze their perceived opportunities has been developed in detail by Schumpeter (1934), and Porter (1980;1985) in particular. The strategy literature on this subject is sometimes called the Positioning School (Mintzberg et al. 1998 p. 82).

91. Literature streams encompassed include Marketing Orientation (Kohli and Jaworski 1990; Noble, Sinha and Kumar 2002), Stakeholder Theory (Donaldson and Preston 1995; Mitchell, Agle and Wood 1997), and Public Policy (Hillman and Hitt 1999; Oliver and Holzinger 2008).

92. This indeed was what Adam Smith expected, and what he called the invisible hand: competitive forces soon lead to virtually all firms converging on the most efficient course of action.

93. There is a branch of literature specifically focused on creating a resource-based advantage over competitors—see Wernerfelt (1984)) and Teece, Pisano and Shuen (1997).

94. This is a theme of the Power and Cultural Schools (Mintzberg et al. 1998 pp. 234 & 264) in particular. See Bower and Gilbert (2007) for some specific examples.

95. Major streams included are Organization Theory (Selznick 1957; Burrell and Morgan 1979) , the Cultural School (Weick and Roberts 1993; Mintzberg et al. 1998 p. 264) and the Power School (Allison 1971; Mintzberg et al. 1998 p. 234).

96. For example, there may be attractive new business areas, or management may find the key group's ethical requirements unduly restrictive.

97. For example, personnel—including the leadership group—nearly always desire greater financial rewards, improved benefits, additional status-symbols, broader discretionary powers, and the opportunity to use the organization's resources to support favored social causes.

98. Useful references include Pfeffer and Salancik (1978) and Pfeffer (1992), though they cover some other channels of influence as well.

99. Alfred Chandler found that companies' strategic decisions were driven by factors other than rational economics. Strategy often stemmed from opportunism, narrow attempts at problem solving, and perhaps fashion trends within the broad business community (1962 pp. v-vii). Chandler's

findings supported both the external and internal social channels of influence. Richard Cyert and James March (1963 p. 117) concluded that the organizations they studied relied on complex internal political processes when they made and implemented decisions. The channel of influence implied was internal-social. Graham Allison (1971) developed three models of decision-making behavior. His first model was the "Rational Actor." This followed outwardly-focused, problem-oriented rational processes (1971 pp. 4-5)—in other words, the external rational channel of influence. His second model was the "Organizational Process Model." He described this as based on the Organization Theory literature's "processes and procedures of the large organizations" (1971 p. 6). His description aligned the model with the internal social channel of influence. His third model was the "Governmental (Bureaucratic) Politics Model," in which the outcome was "a resultant of various bargaining games among players," all of whom are members of the organization concerned (1971 p. 6). Like the second model, this followed the internal social channel of influence. Allison reported that while the first model is the one traditionally used by analysts, the second and third models "provide a base for improved explanations and predictions" (1971 p. 5). Overall, Allison's work mainly supported the internal social channel. Raymond Miles and Charles Snow researched several industries, and found that in all cases an "adaptive" process was followed: the organization noted specific external changes and sought a synergy of (external) environmental forces, (internal) engineering capabilities, and (internal) administrative needs (1978 p. 21). Miles and Snow's work thus supported both the internal social and external social channels of influence. Based on interviews with senior executives, James Brian Quinn (1980 p. 91) found that organizations' managements could make only modest incremental changes to existing corporate directions, and did so by use of extensive internal political processes. Overall, this model described a combination of external rational, external social, and internal social channels of influence.

100. Burrell and Morgan (1979 p. xii) describe the attitude of the holders of paradigmatic views thus: "Whether they are aware of it or not, they bring to their subject of study a frame of reference which reflects a whole series of assumptions about the nature of the social world and the way in which it might be investigated."

101. See Andrews' definition of strategy (1971 p. 28).

102. Alpha's founder's pre-existing personal relationship with potential customers gave the new firm credibility in the external market.

103. If customers must continue to receive the service suppliers produce, and all suppliers offer the same level of service, the customers must accept that level of service. Collectively the suppliers have market power while their

group-solidarity lasts, and Alpha did not need it to last very long. This type of implicit temporary cooperation with competitors is a form of external game-playing.

104. It was a simple defensive strategy focused on covering a weakness in Alpha's resource endowment. The aim was to minimize the duration of the vulnerability, by focusing on accumulating crucial resources. This was an internal issue, resolved by internal action.

105. CEO: Yes, I knew that if I had that machine I would be in front of every other repetition company in Melbourne.

Interviewer: So you knew not only their capability but you (also) knew the market?

CEO: You have to know your opposition.

106. It seems clear that Alpha's strategy relied on rationality. The key question is whether competitors were unable to match Alpha's strategy, or unwilling to do so. If Alpha had market power (i.e., the strategy could not be replicated because of an internal resource that Alpha had and competitors could not obtain), the strategy content would be classified as internal rational. If Alpha did not have market power (the strategy could be replicated but competitors chose not to do so because of a difference in judgment), it would be classified as external rational. It is evident that the difference between Alpha and its competitors was one of judgment. Alpha's strategist was risk-tolerant and favored reinvestment of profits, while competitive strategists preferred less risk and higher dividends.

107. (Chandler 1962; Andrews 1971).

108. (Mintzberg 1972; Mintzberg 1978).

109. (Mintzberg 1978).

110. Each thrust is a single coherent concept and, hence, is conceptually indivisible at the strategic level. (However, it must be implemented through tactical initiatives, so in this sense it can be further deconstructed at the tactical level.) A specific indivisible element of strategy cannot be formed both with and without a conscious strategic decision having been made. If a strategic decision is made but is then fundamentally altered by an emergent process, the final strategy element is emergent.

111. (Mintzberg 1977).

112. (Mintzberg 1978).

113. Figure 1 uses rows (A through D) and columns (1 through 4) to simplify reference to individual processes. For example the first process in Section A occurs in the policy domain, and is therefore called Policy Process A1. The only other process in Section A results in a strategic decision—the

strategist decides whether or not to engage in deliberate strategy formation—so it is termed Strategic Process A2. The left column of sections B and C shows the only two other processes that can occur in the strategic domain—Strategic Processes B1 and C1. All other processes on the diagram are in the tactical domain (B2, C2, D1, and D2), or are purely analytical and involve no decisions or actions (D3 and D4).

114. See Section A of Figure 1.

115. Policy Process A1 prevents the strategist (defined as a person, people or group engaging in or empowered to engage in strategic thinking and decision-making) from taking the organization in a direction contrary to the investors' or members' expectations. It is of course possible that an organization's members will be disappointed by a board's policy decisions. Nevertheless the board's interpretation of the underlying purpose constrains the strategist's available choices.

116. Strategy formation need not be a once-only process; as Andrews (1971 p. 179) and Mintzberg (1987) both emphasized, it can occur recurrently or even continuously in response to changing circumstances.

117. See Section B of Figure 1.

118. See Section D of Figure 1.

119. That is, if Strategic Process B1 has been used.

120. That is, using Strategic Process C1.

121. That is, Tactical Process C2 is broadly similar to Tactical Process B2, but can only occur if Strategic Process B1 was chosen in the previous Section.

122. That is, through Strategic Process C1.

123. That is, Tactical Process D1 could be used.

124. That is, Tactical Process D2 could be used.

125. That is, from Tactical Process D1.

126. That is, if Tactical Process C2 has been used to produce emergent initiatives.

127. That is, the analyst could use Analytical Process D3. Analytical processes do not create strategy; they merely disclose strategy that has already been formed, whether deliberately or emergently.

128. An individual thrust is indivisible at the strategic conceptual level, and cannot stem from both a conscious strategic decision, and the unintended implications of past non-strategic decisions.

129. By using Strategic Process B1.

130. Through Tactical Process B2.

131. By using Analytical Process D4.

132. Interviewer: And you know what kind of business you're going into. Now, how do you get to the next step of "OK I'm going to do this, and I know now is the time"; how do you make a plan, make a commitment?

CEO: ... I think if you can't work it out that, if you've got the contract, then you've got the work (and) well, if you've got the work, if you can supply, you'll stay in business. At the right price.

Interviewer: So, you learned this along the way, or you—

CEO: No, from day one.

133. CEO: Well, there were a lot of people that had dealt with me for six years. And said, "Why aren't you doing it yourself? We'll support you."

134. General Manager: There was a stage (when the CEO) was buying second hand machines, then a time (the CEO) was buying refurbished machines

General Manager: There's a whole lot of differentiation between them immediately at that time, because everyone else is running old second hand machines.

CEO: Yes.

General Manager: ... no maintenance (was) done on (their) machines whatsoever. Here you've differentiated yourself immediately by buying refurbished machines, (because) the quality of the machine (then supports) the quality of the part (being produced). And that's the first thing he's done.

CEO: Yes.

Interviewer: So the first thing you do (is) using effectively the same as everybody else, that is, well, we'll use whatever machine is most affordable, and we'll make products that at least the customer doesn't send back, and that's the way the whole of Australia's automotive industry existed through the fifties and sixties at least?

CEO: Yes.

Interviewer: Now, you start off there, because that's all you can afford to do.

Interviewer: When you make a decision to do something, a commitment—

CEO: Yes.

Interviewer: I'm going to leave here and go to work for myself. I'm going to use refurbished machines instead of old machines. I'm going to get into a serious autolathe here instead of these old single spindle things. Those decisions, was each of those thirty seconds?

CEO: Early in the piece, no; I agonized from day one; I probably agonized for about three months. But then I was unsure of where I was going.

Interviewer: Yes.

CEO: So what I had to do then was make sure that I knew it worked here and here. If this (aspect didn't work), I'll get this one. There was always a plan of attack, where to go.

135. Interviewer: When you bought those (original worn-out autolathes), way back, you didn't differentiate yourself.

CEO: I bought what I could afford.

Interviewer: Yes, but the idea of saying "I can get ahead of the game by going into higher tech equipment, and getting into more design consultation with the customer," these are decisions that happened somehow. How did it happen, was this early or late?

CEO: No, no, it happened very late. I think the single spindle (lathes) down the back was (a case of) buying a machine that I knew I could get work for… (so) that I knew I could survive. Once you survive and own a property and own a building and you've got money in the bank, then you start looking at the new technology.

136. A successful strategist must be able to distinguish between a constraint and the illusion of a constraint (such as a prevailing paradigm). The Alpha CEO was not deflected by illusions, partly because his primary commitment was to acting out his own ego needs, not to conforming to other people's views or preferences.

137. (Andrews 1971). That is, Andrews' model follows Processes A1, A2, B1, C1 and D1 in Figure 1.

138. (Andrews 1971 p. 184).

139. See the Power and Cultural Schools of strategy literature (Mintzberg et al. 1998 pp. 234 and 264). The Power School argues that much of what is allegedly done to implement deliberate strategy actually reflects the separate, even competing, micro-agendas of individuals and sections of the organization. See Bower and Gilbert (2007) for actual examples of this.

140. This is partly because Tactical Process D1 tends to be paralleled unofficially by Tactical Process D2.

141. This is Tactical Process C2. Note that the effects of Process C2 can only be detected by use of Analytical Process D3.

142. Summarized in Mintzberg et al. (1998 p. 176). This specific point is covered in Mintzberg (1987).

143. (Wrapp 1967; Mintzberg 1987).

144. For example see Mintzberg (1985) and Graham Allison's Model III (1971 p. 144).

145. (Wrapp 1967).

146. Wrapp implied that the open-minded strategist routinely carries out Analytical Process D4, and thus becomes aware of the existence and content of the emergent strategy.

147. (Cyert and March 1963). Mintzberg et al. (1998 p. 241) summarized Cyert and March's model as a situation in which "the organization is able to make decisions but it cannot seem to make strategies."

148. (Mintzberg 1987).

149. (Mintzberg 1978).

150. (Bower and Gilbert 2007).

151. (Mintzberg 1978).

152. The full case-study reports I have used are from my doctoral thesis (Chamberlain 2003). Analyzing socially-based case-data in standardized form is challenging for technical reasons. Those who are epistemologically inclined should see Chamberlain (2006) for an explanation of the issues involved and the solution I have adopted. Essentially the technique involves personal immersion in the social situation of one case study at a time. This is followed by importing the specific content of the strategy construct into that case one concept at a time, and testing whether each concept fits the observed reality. The requirements of this process largely dictated the approach to case analysis used in this book.

4
Beta

The nine analysis chapters of this book are structured in four parts: History, First Phase, Second Phase, and Analysis. Analysis consists of classifying the strategist, deconstructing the strategy into components, and classifying each component's content and process. All analysis is based on the tools developed in Chapters 2 and 3. To preserve their privacy I have given the organizations names from the Greek alphabet.

Beta's strategist had to work in a smaller feasible solution zone than Alpha's; the range of potentially successful strategies was heavily restricted by the way the external environment interacted with the strategist's cognitive bias. A valid solution was found and implemented successfully—but to understand its success, we have to recognize the factors that defined the zone.

HISTORY

In 1976, a young man graduated in engineering and immediately took control of Beta, a small second or third tier[153] manufacturing company producing machined metal components in small batches. The firm was founded by his father thirty years earlier. At that time, the firm mainly made parts for farm machinery. However, due to changes in federal government policy, most manufacturing of farm machinery in Australia ceased in the early 1980s and Beta lost its customers. The new CEO found enough new customers to keep the firm alive, but applied no conscious strategy until a few years after his younger brother joined the firm as co-director in 1987. Beta was a small firm with just fifty employees.

THE FIRST PHASE: RECONCILING DESIRES AND OPPORTUNITIES

As in all of the cases in this book, Beta's strategic journey has been divided into two phases. The first phase extends from the elder brother joining the firm as CEO in 1976, to the adoption of a deliberate strategy in about 1991. During the first phase, the CEO did not engage in strategic thinking; he just responded pragmatically to individual problems. A few years after he became CEO, Beta's main customers—farm machinery equipment and component manufacturers, one of which bought 45 percent of Beta's total output—ceased manufacturing, and he had to find new customers. He had some success in this due to the firm's ability to do once-only or low-volume metal-machining jobs at a high quality level—though at a high cost. Over time, he accumulated a group of customers whose needs generally suited Beta's capabilities, but he still avoided drawing conclusions from this and making strategic decisions. He gave two reasons for this reluctance. First, he had no mentor, no one with whom he could discuss and reason. Second, the loss of Beta's sales of parts for farm machinery had happened gradually over several years, and he had not identified a specific crisis impelling him to consider strategy formation. Then in 1987, his brother graduated in engineering and joined the firm. Change followed within a few years.

THE SECOND PHASE: A FOCUS ON AEROSPACE

The CEO's younger brother persuaded him to employ a consultant to help find a specific target market for the firm. The consultant recommended making Beta's special capabilities the focus for market selection. His investigation had shown that Beta's customers recognized the firm as a high capability, high cost manufacturer of small batches of precision-machined metal parts, and he identified the market opportunities that emphasized these qualities—principally, as a third or fourth tier supplier to the aerospace and medical equipment industries. To improve Beta's access to these markets, he recommended obtaining certification under international quality standards. After considering the consultant's report, Beta began to focus on aerospace. The brothers obtained quality certification and US defense supplier accreditation. They also maximized their aerospace component manufacturing capability by deliberately equipping the factory with flexible-application high-technology machines rather than emphasizing low cost per component produced. However, they treated the aerospace focus as a flexible guideline, overruled whenever they saw a business opportunity elsewhere.

ANALYSIS

Classifying the First-Phase Strategist

Change-Readiness

The CEO showed three indications of having an adaptive change-readiness. First, when he took control of the firm in 1976, and again when he began to lose his existing customers about four years later, he did not engage in strategic thinking.[154] He attributed this to not having anyone with whom he could discuss the issues,[155] which seems to indicate a substantial level of self-doubt.[156] Second, when he lost his original customers, he did not make a plan for the business until after his brother joined the company some years later. In the meantime, he looked for replacement customers one-deal-at-a-time, without trying to establish rules-of-thumb based on the experiences he accumulated.[157] This indicates a focus on near-term issues. Third, at no stage during his search did he consider changing the configuration of the firm so it could access a broader market. This reluctance is another adaptive characteristic.[158] Except for these points, he did not exhibit adaptive characteristics to any greater extent than innovative ones. Overall, he seems to have had a mild adaptive preference.

Cognitive Emphasis

Under the typology developed in Chapter 2, cognitive emphasis is determined by the person's imperative: what is the prime consideration when making decisions? Is it materialism (profit and prosperity), egotism (acquiring and exercising an unrestrained power to make arbitrary decisions), or altruism (making a contribution to some humanitarian group or purpose unrelated to the health of the business itself)? It is clear which of these the CEO chose; what he regarded as Beta's essential character was sacrosanct and was not to be changed in pursuit of either commercial success or social contribution.[159] He could have tried to shape the company to suit a mainstream market, but instead he looked for opportunities that suited what he wanted to do, and had become accustomed to doing. This decision was driven by what he called a mindset; he said that he was not interested in work that he considered low technology or dirty. In other words, he granted primacy to personal factors over economic or social ones such as making money or contributing to employment growth. It follows that the CEO was egotistic rather than materialistic or altruistic.

Cognitive Bias

The CEO has been identified as an adaptive egotist, or Operator. The type description in Chapter 2 says that Operators prefer not to adopt strategy or tactics because that would restrict their freedom to make arbitrary operating decisions. They approach operating decisions opportunistically, emphasizing making the deal more than shaping or building the company. This description seems to provide a good fit for the CEO's behavior when he was acting alone in the first phase.

Classifying the Second Phase Strategist

In the second phase, the CEO and his brother/co-director formed a closely-integrated team. Extensive interaction between them led to joint decisions. Interviewed separately, each of them said that his ability to contribute to the process was equal to his brother's. For analytical purposes, the two will be treated as a single gestalt strategist.

Change-Readiness

When surrounded by a strategic vacuum at the beginning of the second phase, the elder brother, already identified as an adaptor, was completely comfortable with the situation. The younger brother was not uncomfortable, but nevertheless responded to an indirect approach from a consultant.[160] In considering the consultant's recommendations, the brothers agreed that the firm's existing configuration was not to be changed,[161] and any strategy would be an advisory guideline, not a basis for decisions.[162] This approach appeals to some adaptive strategists because it enables them to have the comfort of a starting point for decision-making, whilst remaining free to make decisions case-by-case. In other words, the second-phase gestalt strategist seems to have been mildly adaptive rather than innovative.

Cognitive Emphasis

In the second phase, Beta's strategic approach continued to impose the same two requirements as in the first phase. First, the brothers enjoyed doing clean, varied, fairly high technology work and insisted on continuing to do it. Second, they required the freedom to make any decision they wished at any time, without being restricted by a consistent strategy. However, in the second phase, they also added a third requirement: they only wanted engineers as customers' representatives.[163] The character of these three imperatives indicates an egotistic cognitive emphasis.

Cognitive Bias

The second-phase gestalt strategist has now been identified as an adaptive egotist, or Operator. The main change from the first phase was that Beta had a nominal strategic framework rather than simply drifting—but the framework was flexible. Chapter 2 indicates that Operators may prefer to avoid both strategic and tactical decisions, but are happy to make operating decisions as often as necessary. The gestalt strategist matches the Operator type-description reasonably well.

Deconstructing the Strategy

First Phase

Beta's first-phase basic direction was *find new customers without adapting the existing business configuration.* The broad path consisted of one essential thrust: *accept customers opportunistically.* That is, Beta looked for customers who, for whatever reason, would pay its prices and accept the firm as it was. Analyzing his customers' reasons was not a priority for the CEO.

Second Phase

Beta's second-phase basic direction was *focus primarily on aerospace.* The broad path had three essential thrusts: *achieve recognized capability accreditations*; *maximize capability rather than minimizing investment or cost per part*; and *accept non-aerospace customers opportunistically.* This was a more specific strategy than existed at the end of the first phase, though it remained flexible.

Classifying the Strategy Content

First Phase

As explained in Chapter 3, each of a strategy's essential thrusts takes effect through a channel of influence, and there are six types of channels. The only essential thrust in the first phase was *accept customers opportunistically.* This thrust relied on customers self-selecting—Beta's only customers were those who, for some reason, had no real alternative to paying high prices.[164] The channel of influence, therefore, was the broad economic rationality of the external commercial marketplace, so the essential thrust was external rational.

Second Phase

The first of the second-phase essential thrusts, *achieve recognized capability accreditations,* was aimed at making Beta technically acceptable to its intended primary customers (second or third tier aerospace component manufacturers) under the rational selection rules that those customers used. This implies that the channel of influence was external rational. The second thrust, *maximize capability rather than minimizing investment or cost per part,* focused on a critical aspect of how the target customers selected suppliers. Aerospace component manufacturers usually placed orders for packages of different components rather than for individual items, and potential suppliers who could not manufacture every item on the list, and in the prescribed way, were ineligible to bid on the entire package. The aim of the second thrust was to enable Beta to qualify under those selection criteria as often as possible. In other words, it treated the sales process as an external-rational game. The third thrust, *accept non-aerospace customers opportunistically,* was adapted from the first-phase essential thrust. As in the first phase, Beta's opportunism allowed additional customers to self-select by agreeing to pay high prices. This was an external-rational way to test the market continuously and perhaps find new opportunities. In summary, all three essential thrusts were external rational.

Classifying the Strategy Process

First Phase

We classify strategy processes by applying the process model set out in Chapter 3 and illustrated in Figure 1. The model states that the basic direction must be formed either deliberately (B1) or emergently (B2). The CEO did no strategic thinking and took no strategic decisions in the first phase, so the basic direction—*find new customers without adapting the existing business configuration*—must have been formed emergently (B2). That is, the strategy as a whole was not defined by strategic decisions, but has to be inferred by looking at the entire pattern of Beta's management decisions. This implies that the essential thrust, *accept customers opportunistically*, must also be inferred from the pattern of decisions.[165] The whole of Beta's first-phase strategy, therefore, was emergent, and is an example of purely retroactive strategy formation.

Second Phase

The second-phase basic direction, *focus primarily on aerospace*, had to be formed either deliberately (B1) or emergently (B2). In practice, it was recommended by a consultant and adopted deliberately (B1), in what seems to have been Beta's first strategic decision in the entire case study. The first essential thrust, *achieve recognized capability accreditations*, was also recommended by the consultant then adopted deliberately (C1). The second thrust, *maximize capability rather than minimizing investment or cost per part*, expresses an approach that was put into practice later than the basic direction and the first thrust. The CEO indicated that he had gradually learned to do this in order to get orders from aerospace customers.[166] This implies that it had emerged from practical experience rather than being adopted in a strategic decision, so it was originally emergent strategy (C2), but the thrust was later confirmed in a deliberate strategic decision, thus changing its status to deliberate strategy (C1). The third thrust, *accept non-aerospace customers opportunistically*, was originally a piece of emergent strategy carried over from the first phase. However, when asked, the brothers recognized that it was their conscious practice to give precedence to opportunism over the strategy they had stated.[167] Like the second essential thrust, the third had been transformed at some point into deliberate strategy (C1). In summary, the entire second-phase strategy was deliberate.

SUMMARY

In the first phase, the CEO, an Operator or adaptive egotist, did not form strategy. He saw no need for it, and he regarded both strategic and tactical decisions as unacceptably risky unless they could be discussed beforehand with a trusted colleague. This viewpoint offers quite a good match to the Operator type-description.

In the second phase, the CEO and his younger brother established a simple set of strategic guidelines, forming a strategy that recognized the supremacy of opportunism. Subsequently the brothers made no further strategic decisions, and they only made tactical decisions after reaching consensus through extensive discussion. This process, which I have described as decision-making by a gestalt strategist, successfully provided personal satisfaction to the brothers and effective guidance to the business.

NOTES

153. The tier concept was explained in Chapter 1 whilst describing the Alpha case.

154. Interviewer: The two of you in effect worked out where your strengths were, both where you wanted to be and how you could (get) there, what sort of capability you'd have to have to be able to enjoy this vertical distinction, this position you wanted to occupy, and then you had to find customers. Is that the sequence of how this worked, or have I got some of that out of order?

    CEO: No, it's probably not as sequential as you're making it out to be though; it's probably more of an iterative process, a small iteration at a time.

    Interviewer: So it's learning or building in steps or both of those...and it's not so much learning about yourselves as it's learning how the world interacts with yourselves.

    CEO: More so, yes.

    Interviewer: OK. I understand that after you understood where you were as people, you then had to make that match the world by changing what you offered the world until you found something that works.

CEO: Mm.

Interviewer: How much time did it take?

CEO: I've got to think about that. Like, years and years really. Because the market didn't all of a sudden vanish one minute and we ended up in this market the next. ... so I guess it's been a constantly changing process since 1976. Though, I guess more so, the big move (into) defense aerospace really has taken about seven years.

155. CEO: I think working with somebody in an interactive process in decision-making probably means that they're taking some of those decision-tree steps and making sure that you're familiar with the implications of a certain decision, so you probably get a bit more bounce in the decision-making process, working with somebody else with it, you know like if you're getting good interactivity they can bring up another aspect of all of those resources that you've got there at your fingertips to make that decision more correct or not.

CEO: So I had no one as a mentor or a fall-back for over ten years of running the business.

Interviewer: And in that time, this direction then didn't form? Because, I think, you said you formed it jointly with your brother.

CEO: Yes this rapid—oh, not rapid, this I suppose substantial move into defense aerospace didn't really happen until (my brother) came on board and he'd been here probably for five years—five, six, seven years.

156. See Chapter 2 and Appendix 1: innovators are more self-confident, while adaptors are more prone to self-doubt.

157. Excerpt from the original case-study report: "Soon after the CEO took control of the firm, the existing customer base in agricultural and similar industries progressively faded out of existence in Australia. As an ad hoc response to this, the CEO found markets—primarily in the printing and steel industries, but to some extent in precision engineering industries—for (Beta's) metal machining skills."

158. See Chapter 2.

159. Interviewer: You concluded that that was the character of the company—I mean there were two things you could do, you could go to different customers or you could change the company. And you chose to keep the company as it was and go to different customers. Why?

CEO: Probably a combination of things. I'd guess it would be ignorant to say there wasn't a mindset involved in it as well from the directors' point of view. It was the thing that we liked doing. So the idea of the company actually doing a low technology type of application in a dirty environment wasn't really something that we ever really feel comfortable with doing.

So there had to be some sort of directors' vision about what the company would be, and it wasn't that low technology area.

CEO: I think there was a fair recognition of the fact that the strategy of the company would be fairly well at least driven by some emotional factors. We quite recognized that.

160. Younger brother: Well I'd been in the company for about two to three years, and one of my friends—his father was involved with a consultancy group that would look at company strategy business plans...and so I said to (the CEO), suggested to him, look do you want to...this particular fellow, is doing lots of companies like ours, do you want to get him to at least have a talk to us about where our company could be heading; and so one thing led to another and we got him involved.

161. Interviewer: So you've figured out what the company's about and what the directors are about, and, therefore, what business you're going after. Now what did you then have to do? You've got a profile of the kind of customer you want, and you've described the kinds of ones you've found. Did you already know what kinds of production processes you were going to use, and went to find customers who wanted those production processes, or did you learn about the customers, and then define the production processes?

CEO: Probably the first way more than the latter, which probably doesn't make a lot of sense, but that's what we did.

162. Younger brother: Well as I said, it's like a live thing, the strategy. It's not hard and fast and in black and white, it's alive and it moves around. Generally, we're heading in that direction, and then sometimes we find we wander over here and we find that it's going cold, let's go back over here again. So it's really a case of— totally I'd say it's just reacting to market pressures. It's a case of there is a lot of work in this field. If tomorrow somebody came in and said, "Look guys, I can't get this quality work done on steel mill manufacture, I just can't get it done," and if I could see a bit of a market there, that the dollars are in the market, and we had the expertise to do it, well guess where the strategy would be; we'd be starting to go over there, or we might start up another division totally gearing with that.

Interviewer: So the vision is deliberately made the slave of the opportunity rather than the other way around.

Younger brother: That's right, yes.

163. CEO: Yes I think there was a fair recognition of the fact that the strategy of the company would be fairly well at least driven by some emotional factors. We quite recognized that.

Interviewer: And you recognized it at the beginning, or—

CEO: Yes.

Interviewer: It became obvious as you—

CEO: No, no, no, no, we recognized that at the beginning. Because we—I know it sounds a bit strange but well, it sounds really odd to say it but my brother and I are both professional engineers, and when we moved into some areas at the lower technology end of the spectrum, we were dealing with people that we didn't really relate to very well. ..."Well that guy, I don't really understand him, (and) I don't know what he's (talking) about; I don't think we can really help him; he just seems to be on a different wavelength," so we'd say well, if you start to deal with this defense aerospace world, the people that you actually deal with are people like us, so you then feel greater affinity with the client base, and think, "...this suits us, this is our cup of tea." We like dealing with these people, they seem to like us. Let's build on this experience, let's build on this one experience that we had, or two experiences that we had that had proven successful. We've done a good job for them, they like what we do, we can deal with them, and these (are) positive building blocks, so....

Interviewer: Did this happen after you'd decided that you were going in a relatively high tech, high quality direction?

CEO: It would be a parallel process. I guess a company like ours puts out a whole lot of fingers during its corporate lifetime, and sometimes those strategies don't really emerge past the bubble, and other times they get to grow, and they grow because of factors that are there, inherent, and one of those factors would be the emotional feeling of the directors about the strategy.

164. Younger brother: The steel mills would ring up and say, "Will you work all night and make this part for me, because the steel mill's broken down? And we're losing ten thousand dollars an hour." And then you'd pull your crew of guys in, you'd work all night, (come) to work the next morning, (the skilled workers would) take the day off, you'd put your bill in for five hundred, I don't know, a thousand dollars, right, you've done the part within an eight hour time span, which is really good, and then the engineer would ring up and bitch about the price. I said to (the CEO), "I don't want to do that anymore".

165. As explained in Chapter 3, it is logically impossible to make a deliberate strategic decision to adopt an essential thrust in support of an emergent basic direction. If an emergent basic direction is recognized, and adopted deliberately, it becomes a deliberate basic direction. If it is not recognized, deliberate strategic decisions cannot be made in support of it.

166. Interviewer: When you are thinking about new investments, which predominantly I guess is machinery, are there directions that you want to go

in, or is it just a matter of figuring out what the customer wants and saying, "I suppose that's where I've got to go"?

CEO: We always try to make investment decisions such that it improves our (capability)—particularly if we're going for a new technology. Say for instance we're going to buy a five-axis machine tool, we won't buy a little one, we'll buy a big one first. Because that'll do all the jobs that we need to do, and then if we get full (utilization) on that machine then we'll buy a smaller one. So the decision's always about capability, and then capacity. So, just trying to differentiate that way.

Interviewer: You always want more capability because in your very low volume production, the maybe slightly slower cycle time of the big one isn't a disadvantage.

CEO: No, no.

Interviewer: And even the higher capital cost isn't necessarily, because it's so much more important to be able to take the order rather than lose it.

CEO: That's exactly correct. And taking one order means that we can take the raft of fifty other orders that make up that package, but if we can't do one part out of that fifty then, "Oh, we'll go to Fred down the road, he can do the whole package." And all of a sudden we've lost, so having size and differentiators in capability is important for us.

Interviewer: How did you arrive at that conclusion, historically?

CEO: I suppose hitting your head up against a brick wall then realizing that doing it any other way won't work.

167. Interviewer: So the vision is deliberately made the slave of the opportunity rather than the other way around.

Younger brother: That's right, yes.

5
Gamma

There are similarities between the Gamma case and Beta in the previous chapter, but the outcome is different for two main reasons. First, the strategists in the two cases had different cognitive biases. Second, while Beta's strategy was located within a very small strategic solution zone, in Gamma's case, there does not seem to have been such a zone; there may not have been a truly valid solution that simultaneously satisfied the external environment and the strategist's cognitive bias. The Gamma case represents a bridge between Beta (where the solution was perhaps obvious but its recognition was delayed) and the increasingly complex situations in the rest of the book, where in most instances there is no strategic solution zone, just a range of options to choose between—and no strong reason for confidence that any of them will work.

HISTORY

In 1976, a young engineer joined Gamma, a second or third tier component manufacturing business founded, owned, and led by his father. The firm specialized in making metal gears on a jobbing basis—that is, fulfilling individual customer orders for single gears or very small batches. There were essentially two types of customers. The first type of customer consisted of either small firms making complex components which they then sold to machinery manufacturers, or direct sales by Gamma to machine manufacturers. The second type of customer consisted mainly of people repairing or modifying existing machines. The machines involved could be either industrial or agricultural. There was never a specific transition of management from the founder to the next generation, but by 1993, the young engineer had become CEO and strategist. Gamma was a small firm with forty employees.

THE FIRST PHASE: THE OLD ORDER PASSETH

The case has been divided into two phases. The first phase covers the period from the CEO-to-be joining his father's gear cutting firm in 1976, to him eventually becoming strategist in about 1993. Throughout this period, there was no conscious strategy formation at Gamma. Instead, there was continuation of the founder's long-established strategy, which was similar to that of most small manufacturing firms in Australia at that time. The underlying concept was that the federal government applied high import taxes to many manufactured items, thus creating economic opportunities for a multitude of local firms to make these items for the domestic market. Manufacturing volumes tended to be low, resulting in high costs due to lack of economies of scale. This was especially true of Gamma's business, which was largely based on orders for just one or two individual gears. Because so many orders required Gamma's employees to make an item for the first—and possibly the last—time, the formula for success was to use general-purpose gear-cutting machines and employ skilled operators. Each operator would set up a job without special tools or fixtures, make one or two gears, dismantle the set-up, and begin another, unrelated job. To minimize investment, the machines in Gamma's factory were usually acquired second hand and kept in service for as long as possible, perhaps several decades. The diminished accuracy capability of the old machines tended to increase the emphasis on special operator skills. Whenever a particular operator was absent, some customer orders would be delayed. Customers tolerated the high cost, variable quality, and uncertain delivery dates that resulted because they usually had no alternative.

Gamma's first-phase strategy became obsolete after the mid-1980s due to a change in the external environment. The Australian government decided it would gradually remove the import taxes that had been supporting high-cost, low-volume local manufacturing.

THE SECOND PHASE: MAKING GEAR MANUFACTURE VIABLE

By 1993, the new CEO recognized that concentrating on jobbing was no longer viable. As import taxes declined further, most machines that required gears would be imported instead of being made locally, and spare parts for them would be imported from the machines' overseas manufacturers. Some of the local machine manufacturers had stayed in business and continued to buy gears, but to reduce their direct costs (at the expense of higher investment in inventory), they were now tending to buy them in batches of twenty to fifty instead of one or two at a time. Gamma's technology was ill-suited to production in batches, so a major re-equipping program was required. The global trend in gear manufacturing was toward computer numerically controlled machines, so it made sense for Gamma to adopt this technology. However, because of rapid technological change, it was impractical to use second hand computer numerically controlled machines, and new ones cost around US$400,000 each. Gamma could only support that level of investment if it greatly increased its production volume. This implied a radical transformation in work methods, operator skills, and internal culture in the company. Unlike the Beta CEO in the previous chapter, the Gamma CEO had no overwhelming concerns about this. However, he would need to find enough additional work to pay for the expensive new machines, and he did not think he could achieve this by supplying the local market alone, because Australian demand for locally-made gears was declining due to the switch to imported machinery. At the same time, he would not consider making some other product instead of gears, because he was a committed enthusiast in the field of gear manufacture. The only solution to both his economic and egotistic needs seemed to be exporting gears instead of focusing solely on the local market. He believed that this would require upgrading Gamma's capabilities to a world-class level and visibly taking his place on the world stage as a competent and respected gear manufacturer. His strategy to make this transformation had three elements. First, he would change gradually from making gears to individual order, through making them in batches of up to fifty, ultimately to making them in almost continuous production. Second, he would differentiate Gamma within the Australian gear market by becoming the high technology, high capability producer in the same way as Alpha did in Chapter 1. Third, he would join the international community of gear manufacturers, using this group both as a technical resource, and as a source of improved visibility to overseas customers through word-of-mouth communication.

This strategy was ambitious and risky. However, he regarded himself as primarily an engineer and gear-cutting enthusiast rather than primarily a business manager. He acknowledged that he made some of his investment decisions "from the heart" rather than on the basis of economic rationality, and he said that his decision to seek capability leadership in the Australian gear-cutting industry "was a little bit of ego." His general explanation for his approach was, "Us gear people around the world are somewhat passionate about what we do." Nevertheless he was also determined that his stewardship of the family business would be successful.

ANALYSIS

Classifying the Strategist

In the first phase, Gamma's founder was the firm's strategist. By 1976 when the case-study period began, the founder seems to have become strategically inactive, following two decades in a static business environment heavily protected by import taxes. He retired long before the case study interview took place, so he was not interviewed and his classification cannot be analyzed. Only the second-phase strategist—his son, the new CEO—will be classified.

Change-Readiness

The new CEO did some strategic thinking about Gamma's situation and concluded that change was required. He was ready to set aside his firm's culture and even most of its hard-won expertise, replacing all of this with a modern, well-equipped, quality-capable, engineering-oriented firm.[168]

In his interview, he did not spend much time on the disruptions and cultural adjustments that accompany a change of this magnitude; his concerns were technology, capability, and winning personal recognition from his peers.[169] He had a clear vision and made plans calling for Gamma to be updated, expanded, and thoroughly re-oriented.[170] He was focused on the future; to him, what the firm would become was much more exciting than what it would take to get there.[171] He saw the transition as a tactical issue—

it was the outcome that was strategic.[172] This approach—regarding culture and paradigm as barely worthy of comment, and focusing on the vision—is consistent with him being rather innovative.

Cognitive Emphasis

A strategist's cognitive emphasis determines what that person sees as imperative. One thing was imperative to the CEO: making gears.[173] This was more important than how much profit Gamma made, or whether the firm's employees were discomfited by changes that made their existing skills of decreasing relevance.[174] Because his imperative was an ego need, not one based on materialism or altruism, the CEO has been classified as an egotist.[175]

Cognitive Bias

In summary, the CEO was an innovative egotist, or Entrepreneur. His style was conspicuously entrepreneurial; to him Gamma was a vehicle for expressing his will by exercising his enthusiasm and implementing his vision.

Deconstructing the Strategy

First Phase

The basic direction in the first phase remained much the same as it had been when the firm was founded in 1954: *manufacture gears and related items for local customers.* The broad path had three essential thrusts; these were *try to ensure that import taxes remain high, cater to the jobbing trade,* and *use second-hand machinery.* All of these items were the standard strategic approach—indeed the prevailing paradigm—in small Australian manufacturing firms from the end of the Second World War until the high import taxes began to be removed (despite the vehement opposition of most small manufacturers) nearly four decades later.

Second Phase

Gamma's second-phase basic direction was *become a competent gear manufacturer.* The broad path had three essential thrusts: *transition gradually away from jobbing, through batch, to volume production; become the "high technology, high capability" Australian gear manufacturer;*[176] and *network with overseas gear-makers to obtain support and visibility.*[177]

Classifying the Strategy Content

First Phase

We classify strategy content according to which of six possible channels of influence each of the essential thrusts relies upon. In the first phase, the first essential thrust was *try to ensure that import taxes remain high.* The intention of this was to create a market for Gamma's products despite the high prices caused by the firm's lack of economies of scale. From the viewpoint of manufacturers like Gamma, the channel of influence this concept used was rational because it applied economic forces (high federal taxes on competing imports) to force customers to buy from them—a rational customer would accept the best obtainable price whatever it was, as long as it allowed the customer's own business to remain viable. The channel was external because it used an external mechanism (federal taxes) to force customers to pay the high prices. The second essential thrust was *cater to the jobbing trade.* Gamma's potential customers operated on an extremely small scale and wanted to be able to change their product designs on short notice, so they ordered gears on a jobbing basis. This broadly suited Gamma and its competitors, because they lacked the capital to finance batch-oriented machinery. This was an external rational approach; in the game-playing between customers and suppliers, a mutually-satisfactory solution was found. The third essential thrust was *use second-hand machinery.* Because Gamma was focused on jobbing, its production volume was both low and uncertain. The founder, like his competitors, decided that under these conditions it would be excessively risky to expose his firm to the high fixed costs that would result from investing in expensive new equipment. He made this decision whilst knowing that his competitors had made the same choice, so he would save money and reduce risk without suffering a competitive disadvantage. This was the same process of reasoning followed by Alpha's founder in his first phase. By putting all suppliers in the same position, it gave them collectively, but not individually, a form of market power in their game-playing with their customers.[178] It is, therefore, another example of an external rational channel of influence. In summary, all three essential thrusts relied on external rational channels of influence.

Second Phase

In the second phase, the first essential thrust, *transition gradually away from jobbing, through batch, to volume production*, recognized that there was no realistic opportunity for Gamma to succeed as a jobbing specialist in Australia, now that high import taxes were being phased out. Local demand would be too small, and export orders for jobbing work were probably unobtainable because of location issues. The thrust was a risky but economically rational response to a change in the external market, which no longer supported jobbing production of gears. Its channel of influence was, thus, external rational. The second thrust, *become the "high technology, high capability" Australian gear manufacturer*, enabled Gamma to obtain some high volume sales without direct local competitors.[179] This was a similar situation to Alpha's second-phase differentiation strategy; Gamma's local competitors could certainly have emulated what Gamma did, but they chose not to. This, therefore, was an example of competitive game playing, not market power, so the thrust relied on an external rational channel. The third thrust was *network with overseas gear-makers to obtain support and visibility*. This was aimed at making use of external social linkages to improve Gamma's market situation without changing any attitudes or resources in the organization itself. It operated in much the same way as Alpha's first essential thrust in its first phase; the Alpha CEO knew his new business would receive purchase orders, because he had pre-existing positive relationships with his potential customers. Like Alpha's strategic thrust, Gamma's was, therefore, based on an external social channel of influence. In summary the first two thrusts were external rational and the third was external social.

Classifying the Strategy Process

First Phase

We classify each element of strategy as either deliberate or emergent by using the process model set out in Chapter 3 and shown in Figure 1. The first-phase basic direction, *manufacture gears and related items for local customers*, must be either deliberate strategy formed by Strategic Process B1, or emergent strategy from Tactical Process B2. We know that Gamma's first-phase strategy was the same one adopted by most small manufacturers at the time, and was widely regarded as the only practical strategy for such firms. Gamma's founder would have been advised to that effect by both peers and industry associations when he first considered going into business. The basic direction, therefore, was deliberate strategy (B1). The same can be said of all of the three essential thrusts: *try to ensure that import taxes remain high*, *cater to the jobbing trade*, and *use second-hand machinery*. Many small manufacturers deliberately adopted these three thrusts, and regarded them as necessary for survival. The thrusts were therefore deliberate strategy (C1). Thus, the entire first-phase strategy was deliberate.

Second Phase

In the second phase the basic direction, *become a competent gear manufacturer*, once again must have formed deliberately (B1) or emergently (B2). The CEO explained that he gave considerable thought to the strategic issues over several years prior to 1993 before making a deliberate decision.[180] This means the basic direction was deliberate strategy (B1). He also explained how this same lengthy period of strategic thinking produced all three essential thrusts: *transition gradually away from jobbing, through batch, to volume production*; *become the "high technology, high capability" Australian gear manufacturer*; and *network with overseas gear-makers to obtain support and visibility*.[181] All three, therefore, were formed deliberately (C1). Thus, the whole second-phase strategy was deliberate.

SUMMARY

In the first phase, Gamma was strategically inert, perhaps due to having a long-established viable strategy in a static environment. In the second phase, it had a different external situation due to the removal of high import taxes. It also had a new CEO who was an Entrepreneur. As is often the case when an Entrepreneur takes charge, he wanted to make some changes. Changes were required because of the altered external environment, but he may have made bigger changes than were strictly necessary, to satisfy his egotistic objectives. His approach fits the Entrepreneur type description in Chapter 2; he had a vision and it drove him to pursue a path of difficult, discontinuous change. In contrast with this, the adaptive strategists in both phases of the Beta case had no vision; they were dominated by a defensive insistence on preserving the firm's familiar and comfortable configuration. Each of these strategists found a way to satisfy an ego-based personal imperative while also running a business.

NOTES

168. Interviewer: I'm trying to get an understanding of the changes you made—whether you decided to get ahead of the pack, or whether you merely decided you had problems that could be solved by higher technology.

CEO: I've been thinking about this since you rang, and again I can't see a definite decision-making time or a definite decision being made. It was I think a bit of both...it was a little bit of ego...it was partly ego, partly wanting the business to grow and become something worthwhile, but it was also partly from pressure of the type of work and wanting to do quality work. Be able to stand up and—not that I was thinking of it at the time—(do) automotive work, but gee, if you had to do automotive work, you have to have repeatability. These old machines...well, you just can't get the throughput with the old machines. They're manually loaded and you need to do up nuts and bolts and it was just impossible.

169. Interviewer: I mean was this market opportunity driven or was this technology driven?

CEO: I'd say it was technology driven, Geoff.

CEO: So I've come from a nervous engineer who's sort of coming into the shoes of his dad and not known a lot, to where I can stand up in front of a world forum and talk about gears. So, that's achieved one of my goals in life. I want to get the business up there; I want this to be a really viable business and a worthwhile business and something we can make something of down the track.

170. Interviewer: In going from second hand more-or-less manual machines--well, hard automation machines anyway—to CNC machines you deliberately got ahead of the pack. Now when you went first to the old gear grinder and then to a state of the art gear grinder, was that in pursuit of a market opportunity, or was it continuing the direction of being above the technology level in the local industry?

CEO: Yes, a bit of both. Definitely a bit of both.

Interviewer: Does one lead the other? Is it mostly one and the other one helps it along?

CEO: We've got to a stage here where our capability is beyond the local marketplace.

Interviewer: Well, how did that happen? If you were driven by the market, it wouldn't happen I guess.

CEO: No. That's right, that's why I'm saying we're not totally driven by the market. That's why we're pursuing overseas work, because I think our future growth will come from offshore, not from within Australia.

171. CEO: I think mainly my travels and talking to my peers overseas gave me a lot of contacts, I've made a lot of friends world-wide in gear companies. And that's where I saw the opportunity. And again, it comes back to this desire; we've got to do this in Australia. Someone's got to do it or we'll die. In fact, I did media releases when we bought that (computer numerically controlled gear-grinding) machine based on that.

Interviewer: This was driven then by a defensive desire, it wasn't intending to export in the first place.

CEO: No. Definitely not.

Interviewer: They'll do it to us if we don't get the capability ourselves.

CEO: Yes.

Interviewer: And then once you've got the capability, because of scale requirements you're then presumably going to have to export at some point.

CEO: Yes. Yes. We still want the business to grow.

172. CEO: So I was becoming aware of government incentives and so on and so forth through reading technical literature, and I realized there was…well we had problems in this organization. Basically, manufacturing engineering like in gearing as we are, is very capital intensive …with very specialized machines. And when we came to replace some of the older machines the tendency is to replace with used equipment because of the cost of new equipment. And it became a real pain in the late eighties when I realized all the new equipment was getting dearer and dearer, it was all becoming computer controlled. That is CNC controlled.

CEO: The cost of this equipment is so high that you can't justify it just in the jobbing environment. You have to get volume in; you have to get your sales up to help pay for the damn machines. You don't get anything under half a million dollars, and that for us in a little company is a lot of money. So it was technology driven, and once we realized what this could do when we got it in, then we had to work hard to get the volume work.

173. CEO: And we tried in our minds to justify the cost, but in family businesses, you don't really use a lot of sense and sensibility sometimes, it's all from the heart. Mind you, that's typical in the gear world too. Us gear people around the world are somewhat passionate about what we do because it's so unique and different and it's a very, very interesting field of engineering and as I say quite unique, so we get a bit wrapped up in our toys at times.

174. Interviewer: Let's go back. You were making the product, in my words anyway, by dint of great skill rather than great equipment, in the first place, which was characteristic of the early days.

CEO: Yes.

Interviewer: and then you saw a way to produce a more defined outcome where it was not as operator dependent and the equipment itself gave you what you wanted it to do

CEO: That is correct.

And

Interviewer: And you don't want to have a tiny number of people whose incredible manual skills are totally driving your business, and one of those gets a broken leg and you're out of business?

CEO: Yeah, correct.

175. He did not seem to have an interest in advancing the theory of gear design or gear production—his interest was in the practice of the gear-making art. He, therefore, does not seem to have been a theorist (See Chapter 2).

176. Although the CEO adopted the second thrust partly due to (in his words) "a little bit of ego," the decision, nevertheless, also contributed to achieving the basic direction, so it qualifies under Proposition 5 (Chapter 3) as an essential thrust.

177. As in the second thrust, the CEO had an ego-based motivation for adopting this, but the thrust, nevertheless, contributed to achieving the basic direction. Trying to serve technically oriented and sophisticated overseas customers from as far away as Australia would be difficult at best, but should be less so if Gamma had a positive reputation and had good relations with the local gear manufacturers in the target markets.

178. This approach was only feasible because very high import taxes made it uneconomic for customers to import what they needed.

179. CEO: One of our main customers, (an auto industry second tier supplier), for instance, we are the only company that can do the work we do for him. They'd have to buy the machines and equipment themselves to do it, there's no one else in this country to do it.

180. CEO: Since 1993, we have travelled regularly. I probably go offshore once a year myself, if not two or three times, depending on the nature of the travel. This gave me a good picture of what the gear industry was doing around the world, and from there we started to build on our thoughts and ideas. Without sitting down and saying we now have to form a strategy, we learned what our opposition were doing overseas and companies similar to ours, and how they were dealing with it. And we had to—well we did address our own position. So it really was—we hadn't prior to the late eighties or early nineties done anything in the way of strategy building. The business just grew up naturally...natural growth...providing a gear

cutting and gear manufacturing service to local industry. Now in that early nineties period we became world focused.

181. CEO: The danger is that more companies will come in from overseas and just flood us, and put us totally out of business. I wanted to survive, and that was certainly part of the thinking.

Interviewer: So meeting local competition wasn't going to protect you against eventually, overseas competition.

CEO: No.

Interviewer: And your investigation showed that overseas they were doing things that there wasn't a local capability for. So you were vulnerable to people importing the gears instead of getting them locally.

CEO: Yes. Correct.

CEO: We do have a strategy now of networking with everybody we can as a marketing ploy if you like. I've become involved in a lot of associations locally, but we're also members of the American Gear Manufacturers' Association. I attend AGMA, a function every year or every other year. Our company's exhibiting in an exhibition they're putting on for the gear industry in America in October. We did that two years ago, 2001, we exhibited in Detroit. Networking and being part of the engineering community is very much on our agenda and that is a strategic—probably the most conscious strategic decision I've made in the way of future business… obtaining future business.

Interviewer: That's for obtaining business rather than obtaining technical support?

CEO: No, it's both. One's hand in glove.

CEO: In the gear world, we're a family, and you all get to know each other. It's not a big industry, even world-wide it's not a big industry, and we all get to know one another if we go out there. Mind you, I'm the most outward-looking Australian gear manufacturer.

6
Delta

In the first case we looked at—Alpha—the strategist's choices were not severely restricted by the environment. As the firm's founder and sole owner, he decided on an underlying purpose, and then worked out a strategy based to an unusual extent on his own cognitive bias. The Beta and Gamma cases involved more restrictive external environments, so the strategists had to work harder to find solutions that satisfied both them and their environmental circumstances. In this chapter, we see an organization—Delta—facing a set of circumstances that were more like Alpha's, allowing the strategist's cognitive bias again to become an unusually important determinant of strategy.

HISTORY

Delta held a monopoly; it owned and operated a large city's sea port. The organization itself was owned by the state government, and had invested in the required plant and equipment to make the port reasonably capable and efficient. The port was on the edge of the city center, which resulted in Delta owning a large amount of inner-city waterfront land that it used only for port operations. Until a few years before the case study, Delta's predecessor, a state government authority, had employed thousands of people and engaged directly in cargo-handling. Then an economically-rational, reformist state government converted a number of state-owned organizations—most of them infrastructure monopolies like

Delta—into government-regulated commercial businesses with a profit motive. The intention was that the state government would manage any public policy matters the monopolies had previously handled, and the newly-commercialized organizations would be regulated to keep them from raising prices excessively. This would leave increases in efficiency and throughput as the only ways these new businesses could enhance their profits. After being reorganized in this way, the port authority's shore-based activities became Delta, which was still asset-rich, but now employed only eighty people. It leased complete cargo-handling facilities to privately-owned stevedoring firms, each of which loaded and unloaded ships for shipping companies. Shortly before the case study, a shift in political climate had seen the reformist government replaced by a more traditional one with less appetite for change and controversy.

At the beginning of the case study period, a newly appointed CEO took charge of Delta. He inherited a mission statement, and a strategic plan prepared immediately before his arrival. He disagreed with both mission and plan. The crucial issue was whether Delta was to be a business or a piece of public infrastructure. As a business, Delta would be a commercial company driven by financial and efficiency objectives, but one which just happened to be owned as well as regulated by the state government. As infrastructure however, Delta would be a quasi-autonomous government-owned organization, which just happened to have a corporate structure. The incoming CEO held the view that Delta was infrastructure, while the mission statement and strategic plan said it was a business. Delta's board did not seem to have a specific position on the issue. Although Delta had only eighty employees, I have classified it as medium-sized because of its relatively large asset base.

THE FIRST PHASE: GETTING THE RIGHT MISSION STATEMENT

As in all of the cases in this book, Delta's strategy development has been divided into two phases. The first phase consisted of the CEO's initial eight weeks, when he intended to transform the organization in the minds of its employees from a business into a piece of infrastructure. In the second phase, he wanted to revise Delta's approach to reflect the infrastructure concept.

The mission the CEO inherited was focused on company profitability, and while he did not object to making a profit and paying a moderate dividend to Delta's owner (the state government), he saw that as a minor, nearly trivial matter. It was completely clear to him that the true purpose of any state-government-owned port was to build up the state's economy. As far as he was concerned, Delta was not there to be a landlord; its real function was to oversee a large-scale essential service. A specific, important issue in Delta's case was that various promoters and investors wanted to convert as much as possible of the organization's land into premium commercial and residential waterfront development projects. The CEO believed that this was incompatible with Delta's true, service-oriented mission, and he intended to resist the developers' desires. Given all of this, the CEO felt that describing Delta's mission as maximizing its profitability as a landlord simply missed the point.

Not only did the CEO inherit an unacceptable mission, he had to replace that mission in just eight weeks, before Delta's new strategic plan was due to be submitted to the state government. He wanted to be surrounded by a team of supportive, committed people rather than personally commanding and controlling the organization, so he needed to win the management team over to an infrastructure mission. This was his strategic focus in the first phase.

He approached the mission-change project by using his own version of the Socratic method of inquiry. For several weeks, he met with his staff both individually and as a group, in the guise of being a new CEO trying to familiarize himself with the business. He asked a series of targeted questions, already knowing the answers he wanted. When he thought the required ideas had taken root, he asked the staff to consider a new mission statement centered on "promoting the sustainable economic and social development" of the state by "providing the best-connected port in Australia." This mission positioned Delta as infrastructure, and had little or nothing in common with the profit-centered mission it replaced. The CEO's influence technique succeeded, and the mission change was accepted within the eight-week period.

THE SECOND PHASE: ACTING LIKE CORPORATIZED INFRASTRUCTURE

After the new mission statement was adopted, the CEO had the broader, but less time-constrained, task of getting Delta's people thinking and working like an infrastructure organization. This meant changing objectives and methods so that the revised mission actually dominated the organization's activities.

In the second phase, the CEO was concerned about three threats. The first was other ports poaching the shipping companies currently using Delta's port. The second was land developers taking over some of Delta's real estate. The last was city residents lobbying for tighter limits on the port's noise emissions, operating hours, and truck movements. In dealing with these matters, he aimed at making Delta an active, influential participant in its own right, rather than relying entirely on the state government to deal with such issues. In effect, he divided the external environment into competitors (other ports), adversaries (property developers, city residents, and the state government's profit-emphasizing financial department), and allies (shipping companies, local railways, and any significant government departments sympathetic to Delta's new mission). He intended to act issue-by-issue to out-maneuver competitors, frustrate adversaries, and build ever-stronger interdependencies with allies.

The CEO believed the port's future contribution to the economy would be greatest if Delta itself became effective in winning new business for the port. He decided that the key to achieving this was for Delta to have access to intelligence both on a broad front and deal-by-deal, so that he could use the information to make the organization a player rather than a landlord. To achieve his intent, he needed to make three changes. First, gathering and analyzing intelligence had to become Delta's most-emphasized continuous business process. Second, the internal culture had to become aligned with his approach of dividing the active, influential participants in the world of ports and transport into competitors, natural adversaries, and business allies. Third, to make the port sustainable, Delta's managers needed to consider the future as well as the present when making investment decisions. He set out to implement this strategy by a combination of techniques. He gathered intelligence by forming a personal network of business partners, especially shipping company executives. He also made intelligence-sharing a focus of his management meetings, thus increasing the prestige of staff who contributed information. He implemented the other two changes through psychology-based leadership techniques enabled by his genuine intellectual advantage and his aura of authority as CEO.

ANALYSIS

Classifying the Strategist

The case analysis process begins with assessing the strategist's cognitive bias using the typology from Chapter 2. Delta's strategist was the CEO.[182]

Change-Readiness

To assess change-readiness, we rely on the distinctions between adaptors and innovators set out in Chapter 2. In the case of the Delta CEO, the most easily-observed signs—whether he preferred incremental or discontinuous change, was risk-averse or risk-tolerant, and made all decisions after deliberation or sometimes decided impulsively—do not seem to point clearly either way, though there was certainly no indication of impulsiveness. This probably means he was not markedly either adaptive or innovative, but was close to the population mean. To classify him we, therefore, have to resort to more subtle indications. The main clues lie in three points. First, while he wanted to change the organization's course, his new direction was not a novel one; it was a reversion to the way government-owned ports, including Delta's, had traditionally been managed in Australia.[183] Second, one of the aims of his actions was to put himself on familiar ground, with intelligence to hand, political networks in place, and a supportive team that shared the paradigm he insisted on bringing with him to Delta.[184] To achieve this he patiently spent time on consensus-building.[185] This suggests that it was fairly important to him to avoid being in an isolated position. Third, while he wanted his team to look several years into the future for facilities planning, he based the planning process on what the cargo handlers and shipping companies requested; he did not have a vision for the port.[186] Delta's strategy manager said that the organization was reactive to the needs and demands of its business partners. He also said that the leadership team believed this to be the appropriate stance.[187] Putting these three points together, it seems that the CEO may have been slightly adaptive.[188]

Cognitive Emphasis

Distinguishing between various cognitive emphases requires identifying the strategic imperative that ranks ahead of any other consideration when the person makes decisions. As indicated in Chapter 2, materialists maximize income, egotists maximize their own power, and altruists create value for some group deemed worthy—the human species as a whole or a specific subgroup.

The CEO made it clear that while he was willing to pay a reasonable dividend to Delta's owner (the state government),[189] his imperative was to foster trade and create economic advantage for the state's residents.[190] He certainly was not interested in maximizing the organization's profit—he did not regard profitability as the most significant aspect of Delta's performance.[191] His resistance to focusing on income-generation objectives was so strong that he regarded the state government's revenue and expenditure department as an enemy to be resisted and thwarted.[192] He had held this attitude ever since his previous job working for a different state government.[193] This indicates that he was not a materialist. On first inspection, his focuses on creating influence for the organization he headed, and ensuring that the organization responded to his leadership, could be characteristic of an egotist. However, an egotist would regard the power as an end in itself rather than a means to an end. The Delta CEO put himself into a very strong position in the organization—he dominated his staff intellectually,[194] and manipulated them psychologically—but he did not revel in making powerful, visible decisions, and did not seem to have difficulty making genuine delegations of authority. His primary attitude—crusading for the interests of a specific group of people he had adopted as a personal constituency—indicates that he was an altruist.[195]

Cognitive Bias

These observations mean that the Delta CEO's cognitive bias—his combination of change-readiness and cognitive emphasis—was adaptive altruist. This is the type I called the Administrator in Chapter 2. The CEO seems to fit the profile satisfactorily, including his strong adherence to the aim of creating economic growth rather than profits, and his desire to be included in a group consensus (though he worked hard to obtain a consensus consistent with his own views).

Deconstructing the Strategy

First Phase

The CEO, having judged that it was important to adopt a new mission before submitting the business plan, made that the basis for his first-phase strategy. In other words, his basic direction was *win internal acceptance for an infrastructure mission.* This was a simple basic direction, and the distinctive path was correspondingly uncomplicated, having just one essential thrust: *ask leading questions.*

Second Phase

The second-phase basic direction can be summarized as *make Delta an influential participant which achieves a positive local impact.* There were three essential thrusts in the distinctive path. First, Delta had to *continuously obtain high quality intelligence.* Second, it had to *routinely regard certain groups as business partners, competitors, and adversaries.* Finally, Delta had to *adopt a long-term approach in planning facilities and linkages.*

Classifying the Strategy Content

The next step is to identify the channels of influence that were to make the strategy effective.

First Phase

Delta's only first-phase essential thrust, *ask leading questions,* was applied internally as a form of psychological manipulation and, therefore, used an internal social rather than a rational channel.

Second Phase

The first of the second-phase essential thrusts was *continuously obtain high quality intelligence.* This meant obtaining external intelligence to use externally, in a process of rational game-playing. This, therefore, used an external rational channel. The second thrust was *routinely regard certain groups as business partners, competitors, and adversaries.* This was setting up the structure for external game-playing by assigning the external players to teams based on rational criteria. It, therefore, can be classified as external rational. As the third thrust, Delta had to *adopt a long-term approach in planning facilities and linkages.* The CEO's objective was to create a sustainable capacity to serve the state's people.[196] His intention was to listen to shipping companies and other partners, then plan in line with their expressed needs.[197] That is an externally-focused economic process based on rational actions. To summarize, all three essential thrusts were external rational.

Classifying the Strategy Process

First Phase

The strategy process model shown in Figure 1 tells us that the first-phase basic direction, *win internal acceptance for an infrastructure mission,* must have either been deliberately chosen (B1) or arrived at emergently (B2). In practice the CEO made it clear that he chose it deliberately (B1).[198] Following Figure 1, the next step is to identify whether each essential thrust was chosen deliberately (C1) or emergently (C2). There was only one essential thrust, *ask leading questions,* and the CEO once again made it clear that he chose it deliberately.[199] Thus, all of the first phase strategy process was deliberate.

Second Phase

The second-phase basic direction, *make Delta an influential participant which achieves a positive local impact,* again, must have been adopted either deliberately (B1) or emergently (B2). It is evident that the CEO brought a general inclination of this nature with him when he joined Delta—it was something he had worked out during his prior experience with another state government. When he arrived, he was consciously sure that Delta existed to have a positive local impact. After arrival, he concluded that passivity was not a viable option when there were competitors and adversaries to defeat. This view and his supporting reasons were evident in his interview.[200] The choice was thus a result of strategic thinking, though some of that thinking predated his appointment to Delta. It follows that it was deliberate strategy (B1).

Referring again to Figure 1, each of the three essential thrusts supporting the deliberate basic direction must have arisen either deliberately (C1) or emergently (C2). The CEO saw the first thrust, *continuously obtain high quality intelligence*, as the key strategic issue.[201] Therefore, it was deliberate strategy (C1). The second thrust, *routinely regard certain groups as business partners, competitors and adversaries*, was implicit in much of what the CEO said and did.[202] It was a conclusion based partly on his prior experience, and partly on conscious strategic thinking after he joined Delta. It must, therefore, be classified as deliberate strategy (C1). The third and last thrust was that Delta had to *adopt a long-term approach in planning facilities and linkages.* This was chosen in a conscious, explicit strategic decision by the CEO.[203] It was therefore deliberate strategy (C1). In summary, all elements of the second-phase strategy were deliberate.

SUMMARY

The case emphasizes the importance of the strategist's cognitive bias. This strategist's cognitive emphasis—altruism—may be unusual in commercial businesses, for reasons that should be obvious after reading the case analysis. Boards of directors and the company regulatory system are geared to oversee CEOs to ensure they do not take financial advantage of their positions or abuse their personal power, but the system is not well-adapted to deal with a CEO who will not favor shareholder interests. Whether this CEO was suitable for his job at Delta depends on the organization's underlying purpose—in particular, whether Delta was a commercial business or a piece of public infrastructure. The normal business process would have been for Delta's board to answer that question when it selected and instructed him, but apparently this was not done, or at least not in sufficiently clear terms. The outcome was that the strategist, rather than the owner or the board, determined the organization's underlying purpose.

NOTES

182. Interviewer: Now, my first generic question is what person or persons in the company propose strategy, and I think you've explained that. At the very highest level, it's predominantly you, but it rapidly fans out.

CEO: Hmm. I'd say I provoke it. That's my style, yes, but I've usually got a number of ideas, which I've various degrees of self conviction about. But I always want to take people with me. And take me through that process.

183. This includes the ports he had personally worked with in his previous job. The CEO had been a senior civil servant helping set transport policy in another state, and had been involved in a cabinet discussion on the subject:

CEO: And I remember doing a cabinet briefing and saying in response to a question from the premier—and it wasn't in the brief—I said, "At the end of the day Premier, I actually believe that ports are there to facilitate trade." And he said "That's it. That's what the Act's got to be about."

(Note: premier is the Australian term for a state governor.)

184. CEO: We're not the economic development arm of government, of state and regional development. The unique way that we contribute to that, or promote that—we're not the sole management—when we talk about promoting the sustainable economic and social development of the state, we do it by providing the best-connected port in Australia. There's a lot of nuances in best-connected I might add. I'll elaborate that if you like. That's not just physical connection, it can be information connection, people connection, and my word that's been one of the most powerful parts of that purpose statement. It's talking about the best-connected port in Australia. I ask people to hang on for that because connected can mean shipping line services, it can mean information flows, it can be your road and rail network, it can be your people network, and that's proved enormously powerful. Just as a motivator. Sustainability's proven a very good motivator, but best-connected, there's so many dimensions to that, not just infrastructure.

185. CEO: So I was only able to do so much in the first year—we had a requirement and they'd done all the usual corporate retreats and so on and so forth, and it came to me within eight weeks of when it was due for submission, and I realized that it was too inward-looking and so on, and I was the new boy on the block; and you had to be quite careful, there was a very high level of ownership.

CEO: So I did it by a process of inquiry, and I said that's fine, that's something we do, something government wants to do, they're the shareholder, they're entitled to a dividend, I didn't have any problems with any of that. But we just had—and this is to be honest only at the executive team, the team that I was still just getting used to…and it fairly quickly came out that no, no, no, they said, "Give them ten million dollars, but we're a key part of the economy." I led it in. I mean, to be honest—and I wouldn't want to liken myself to it but—I mean you probably know in the classics how Socrates actually got people to come up with the answer themselves by asking questions, he never told them what the answer was but he got an answer and he asked them another question…it's more by inquiry and questioning.

186. CEO: And you know, there are plenty of companies I'm sure which have been helped by that vision and insight, but there are also plenty of others where they believed they had the vision and insight and got it hopelessly wrong.

Interviewer: Yes, that's right.

CEO: Hopelessly wrong, on the wrong planet as it were, but they had a vision, and they had an insight; they were as convinced as the people who got it right, but actually, they got it wrong.

187. Strategy Manager: You're probing for where do ideas come from.

Interviewer: Yes.

Strategy Manager: … I think because we feel we're a service organization, we think we're facilitating the initiatives of others. Innovation and ideas is not perhaps uppermost in our minds. We're not structured as an ideas…leader.

Interviewer: Customer driven?

Strategy Manager: Yes, we're customer driven. I think we're obliged from our charter to manage this facility as efficiently and as customer-focused as we can. It doesn't really lead to and it doesn't reward ideas generation. That's not to say that people don't use their initiative within that.

188. When I wrote Delta's case study report (the second in a series of ten, written immediately after interviewing the CEO and Strategy Manager), I suggested that the CEO was very slightly innovative. While further experience has changed my view, I still believe there was no strong evidence to identify him as either adaptive or innovative. A person close to the population mean may show a mild form of both adaptive and innovative characteristics.

189. CEO: And I said that's fine, that's something we do, something government wants to do, they're the shareholder, they're entitled to a dividend, I didn't have any problems with any of that.

190. CEO: That's the exciting part of the business, it's not particularly gratifying or exciting to send a check off to a treasurer. What's far more exciting is to talk to the Farmers' Federation and to give them a competitive edge in the world market, say to the Middle East as we were doing in (the state he worked for previously) for example, by doing something in your port or helping them with something in the transport linkages.

(Note that treasurer is the Australian term for the elected cabinet member responsible for revenue, often called the finance minister in other countries.)

191. CEO: Because at the end of the day, we might give Treasury ten million dollars, but ten million dollars in the state budget, that doesn't buy many schools, you know, probably build one and a half primary schools, or something like that, so is that why government has us here?

192. The department that taxes, spends, budgets, and manages the economy in Australian state governments is called the Treasury.

CEO: Treasury, of course, was apoplectic.

CEO: And so it was just resonance at the time, so that a convenient turn of phrase netted a good way of foiling Treasury, as it were.

193. CEO: And that took us back to the fundamental question of why do we have a port. I mean you can't write legislation without working out—whether you call them objectives or purposes of the Act or whatever word you put round it—why do we have a port? And there was a very strong school of thought, driven by Treasury, that they are revenue generators. There was an alternative school of thought, which was strong in my department, the Department of Transport, and strong in my thinking—they were not revenue generators, they're economic generators. And this was a battle that we fought for a long time within government before it went to cabinet.

194. Strategy Manager: The CEO (CEO's name) is intellectually in a different league to all of the rest of us. He's very quick at conceptualization and very quick to problem-solve, and see strategies and see directions.

195. CEO: So, in a sense, it's almost blindingly obvious that, that's why you're there. Because if you didn't have exporters or importers and those shipping lines, well the stevedores wouldn't bother to be here, there's nothing to load and unload, so you won't have tenants there wanting to offer services. So it is very much what we do on a day to day basis; it's a relationship with people who take a lease on land so they can provide some sort of service, and who actually work with the cargo owners saying, come out through this port, and we'll work with the shipping lines who call at this port, and you marry them up, that is really what ports do. And I say, within an organization that's far more motivating than putting an extra million in the dividend check or something like that. And we'd get a great kick out of some of the success stories of new markets for exports from some of the back blocks near (a rural city), something like that. And working with the road carriers or the rail carriers or whatever, so that is manifestly why you have ports, it's for trade.

196. CEO: I had a belief that one of the reasons, the primary reason, why we have statutory authorities within government rather than privatized things…is not just so it works today, the port works today, but I started saying to my people "If (Delta's port) has problems in ten years' time—if it can't cope with growth or if it's got all the neighbors offside, whatever it happens to be and those are the sort of things—or we haven't got the right sort of infrastructure coming in and out, whatever it happens to be, we'll have failed. And that is one of the reasons that government actually have us here…to do that planning, and investment, and all those other sorts of things to ensure that the port will be working in ten years' time, and we

will have failed if the problem is huge in ten or twenty or thirty years' time and through that, the issue of sustainability.

197. Strategy Manager: Yes we're customer driven. I think we're obliged from our charter to manage this facility as efficiently and as customer-focused as we can. It doesn't really lead to and it doesn't reward ideas generation. That's not to say that people don't use their initiative within that.

198. CEO: I realized that it was too inward-looking and so on, and I was the new boy on the block, and you had to be quite careful, there was a very high level of ownership.

199. CEO: So I did it by a process of inquiry…I led it in…and it happened over a period of a few weeks, and I at one stage just popped the question, and said, hey, what if we actually say the reason we are here is really to support the social and economic development of the state?

200. CEO: Talk about the high-level purpose…state government, pay them a nice dividend…I challenged that, because I don't—when I came here I was able to do that—I just don't believe that's the reason we have ports.

CEO: And that has driven all sorts of things because where it previously was a sort of unidimensional—well, single bottom line financial—and it wasn't even sustainable financial it was just plenty of profit. It wasn't even thinking about what infrastructure we need to do in the next ten or twenty years given the growth we expect to happen, and can we self-finance, what's our financial strategy, how highly geared should we be, all those sorts of things. So it brought new dimensions in there, it brought about an enormous suite of (plans) about really ensuring we have the license to operate in the community and re-linking, reconnecting the port with the community. And it's also brought about a much more fulsome suite of (plans) in terms of the physical environment sustainability, green targets and so on. It's also brought about some other interesting in-house things and the way the values have emerged and so on.

201. CEO: I think, to be honest, the key driver for us right now is internal knowledge and information. And we can do that because we are extraordinarily well connected with major customer groups, and the flow of information is nothing short of stunning and sensational in terms of the confidential information that we come across, the trends that are happening in their worlds that we pick up, we are very well connected.

202. CEO: First of all, what are other ports up to, in terms of trying to seduce customers away.

Interviewer: But you also wouldn't have to change the purpose statement to say that the river front, which you currently occupy, and use in varying degrees of intensity along the river, may or may not become or ought to become, multi-purpose, or integrated, or there are lots of visions that could occur.

CEO: Yes, you could put some restaurants along there, yes.

Interviewer: Some people want to do that I understand.

CEO: Yes, well we've already got one, which is a tragedy, but anyway.

CEO: So that means then, that we would only do things like putting lots of restaurants along there or whatever else we might do, if it was consistent with or not inimical to having the operations of the base port in (this city)...which it is. So those sorts of things are not part of our agenda because we'd be compromising the port, as a functioning entity.

CEO: If we wreck the environment there'll be a lot of pressure on us to move out of here. But also importantly, very importantly in the port situation in terms of our interaction to the community, because if you look at capital cities around the ports, they're all getting squeezed by the growing population. I mean, you can see we've got moved out of (a large city redevelopment on former Delta land) and are being squeezed downriver and so on...but it's the community's tacit willingness to let you continue, not putting political pressure on to limit hours of operation or less noisy machinery, or heaven help us, move it off the bay, really somewhere else.

CEO: And that took us back to the fundamental question of why do we have a port. I mean you can't write legislation without working out—whether you call them objectives or purposes of the Act or whatever word you put round it—why do we have a port? And there was a very strong school of thought, driven by Treasury, that they are revenue generators. There was an alternative school of thought, which was strong in my department, the Department of Transport, and strong in my thinking—they were not revenue generators, they're economic generators. And this was a battle that we fought for a long time within government before it went to Cabinet.

CEO: Treasury, of course, was apoplectic.

CEO: And so it was just resonance at the time, so that a convenient turn of phrase netted a good way of foiling Treasury, as it were.

203. CEO: I had a belief that one of the reasons, the primary reason, why we have statutory authorities within government rather than privatized things...is not just so it works today, the port works today, but I started saying to my people, "If (Delta's port) has problems in ten years' time—if it can't cope with growth or if it's got all the neighbors offside, whatever it happens to be, and those are the sort of things—or we haven't got the right sort of infrastructure coming in and out, whatever it happens to be... we'll have failed."

7
Epsilon

Epsilon, a large not-for-profit industry association, was affected by a radical change in its external environment that would eventually invalidate some of its main functions. Most of the association's members wanted to resist the environmental change, but eventually the CEO concluded that this was not a viable posture. The case study concerns Epsilon's transition to a new posture and strategy.

HISTORY

In the mid 1980s, the Australian federal government began to phase out a long-established practice of protecting small local manufacturers by imposing high taxes on imported items. Most of the protected manufacturers saw this policy change as supremely threatening, and opposing and resisting it immediately became the highest-priority task of Epsilon, a large industry association focused on the manufacturing sector of the economy. Epsilon engaged continually in vigorous, often emotional, public campaigning in support of retaining high import taxes.

The most important reason for Epsilon's existence was labor relations, which were dominated in Australia by a court process. Traditionally, Epsilon's key service to its members was managing the employers' side of this, both for individual firms and more importantly, for the manufacturing industry sector collectively. From 1990, the federal government moved to reduce the importance of this legal process by partly replacing it with collective bargaining.

Epsilon's economists predicted that if high import taxes were removed, one of the consequences would be that the court-based wage-fixing process would become impractical, and would have to be eliminated almost entirely. This second change in government policy was of great importance to Epsilon, because while it would not have harmed the members, it could have harmed the association itself. By eliminating the members' need for the association's premier service, it would eliminate their need to be members. Epsilon's own self-interest as an organization, therefore, aligned with its members' desire to retain high import taxes.

Over nearly a decade of Epsilon's ongoing, strong agitation against the federal government's policy of reducing import taxes, the association's relations with the government were adversely affected. Meanwhile a minority of the association's members, including some with seats on its governing council, came to accept the import tax reductions as inevitable and restructured their businesses accordingly. This split the membership into two groups on the import tax issue. Epsilon's own staff was also split, based largely on how individual departments would be affected by the two ongoing shifts in government policy. Eventually, Epsilon's strident and trenchant stance on import taxes caused it to be in danger of losing access to the top stratum of government. Epsilon was a medium-sized organization with a staff of two hundred.

THE FIRST PHASE: AVOIDING THE THREAT OF IRRELEVANCE

As usual, the case will be divided into two phases for analysis. The first phase begins in January 1994 when the CEO made a personal decision that Epsilon would cease supporting high import taxes. It ends with his retirement in 1996. The second phase begins with the accession of a new CEO, and runs until the case study was conducted in 2003.

At the beginning of the first phase, Epsilon was in an untenable strategic position due to having been guided by short-term thinking. Most members were strongly opposed to reduced import taxes. The association's underlying purpose was to pursue the members' interests, so its own democratic processes, supported by its own organizational interests, had painted it into a corner. However, in January 1994, it became clear to the CEO that Epsilon's position had to change. Years of public agitation and private lobbying, across several federal elections, had not shifted the government's policy. At some point the association had to recognize that further resistance was counterproductive to its own and its members' interests. The strategy the CEO chose for extracting Epsilon from this quagmire was centered on protecting the association from further damage. He attempted to do this by making three decisions. The first was that he would reverse Epsilon's position and support the gradual removal of the high import taxes. The second was that he would announce the association's policy change at a high-profile public event as soon as possible. He wanted considerable publicity because that was likely to make Epsilon's policy change irreversible, thus minimizing the risk of a disruptive member-revolt after the announcement. The third decision was that he would take personal responsibility for the change in policy. He was approaching retirement age, so he could retire as soon as the uproar following his announcement had receded, thus leaving his successor with a clear field.

The strategy was executed successfully. He obtained the agreement of Epsilon's governing council more easily than he expected, then announced the position reversal in a public lecture that he delivered in May 1994. He suffered the outrage of many of Epsilon's members, and public ridicule from federal politicians who had been offended by his previous recalcitrance, until he retired in 1996. By then the emotion had receded and his successor's strategic options were as open as possible.

THE SECOND PHASE: SUSTAINABLE STRATEGIC CONCEPTS

The new CEO began his strategic thinking before he came to office. He had been troubled for several years by the emergence of a new style of industry association based on the concept of fee-for-service. Historically, industry associations had represented every member's interests across a wide range of situations as a basic entitlement covered by the ordinary membership fee. This captured as much as possible of the representational work for the associations' own staffs, thus achieving economies of scale in their service departments. The new fee-for-service associations charged only a nominal membership fee, but then any required service came at a price. The fee-for-service concept could drive a wedge between those members who tended to make use of the services, and those who did not. This would potentially divide the market for industry association membership, thus eliminating Epsilon's economies of scale, which had previously been an important barrier to the creation of new, competing associations. In a fragmented market, Epsilon would no longer be able to claim convincingly to speak for its entire sector, and much of its influence, visibility, and access to government would be lost. Based on this reasoning, the CEO concluded that Epsilon must continue to be a large full-service industry association, regardless of what its competitors did. He concluded that this strategic direction could be viable if he took two steps. First, more members must be acquired. This would maintain Epsilon's economies of scale despite inevitable membership losses when some existing members either chose fee-for-service, or decided they no longer needed association membership once collective bargaining replaced the traditional court process. Second, to maintain Epsilon's influence, access to government, and the attractiveness of membership, the association must market itself more effectively. This required a combination of improved branding and attractive, highly-visible new services.

The economies-of-scale initiative was pursued by a combination of merger with another association almost as large as Epsilon itself, and vigorous ongoing membership drives. The marketing measure involved creating and publicizing a new brand for the merged association, and tying it to a series of services organized by the economics department. These services consisted mainly of Epsilon running regular economic-forecasting conferences featuring well-known economists, and releasing professionally-conducted quarterly economic surveys of the ten thousand manufacturing firms that were its members. The survey results became significant sources of national economic data, with attendant publicity each time they were released. Based on the visibility stemming from these activities, Epsilon strengthened its existing position as the usual spokesperson for manufacturing industry, and became more visible and credible as an economic commentator.

ANALYSIS

Classifying the Strategist

The first-phase CEO had been retired for six years when the case study was conducted, and because of that he was not interviewed. The only strategist whose cognitive bias will be classified is the second-phase CEO.

Change-Readiness

The second-phase CEO spoke of himself as the steward of the organization, and referred to his pride in Epsilon's long history.[204] He emphasized that the association nearly always promoted staff from within rather than recruiting externally.[205] These points suggest an adaptive preference. A stronger indication, however, comes from his approach to strategy formation. He introduced his strategic changes in response to recognized, pressing external threats, and the changes themselves were aimed at preserving as much of the existing configuration as possible.[206] The type descriptions in Chapter 2 observe that preferences for not forming strategy except when under threat, and for avoiding changes in the organization's configuration, tend to be associated with adaptors. Innovators are more inclined to search for new opportunities without the stimulus of threats. Furthermore, the CEO did not have a vision, as an innovator usually does; instead he had concerns and considered what responses he would make to them. It appears that he had a mild adaptive preference.

Cognitive Emphasis

The CEO measured the quality and stability of industry associations by the extent of their annual financial surplus or deficit.[207] As part of his financial oversight of Epsilon, he introduced a number of measures to improve budgeting and efficiency.[208] This emphasis suggests that he was a materialist. He was clearly not an egotist, because he put his deputy into a position of high public visibility by allowing her to organize and present Epsilon's strategically important economic conferences and member economic surveys without his own involvement. He also showed no signs of being an altruist. His primary personal focus was on stewardship and the viability of his organization, rather than national economic outcomes or the financial health of his members. To him the term strategy meant association strategy, not manufacturing-industry strategy.[209] It appears the CEO was a materialist, not an egotist or altruist.

Cognitive Bias

The CEO has been identified as an adaptive materialist, or Executive. His strategic approach was essentially to preserve Epsilon's size, viability, and influence without any avoidable change in basic configuration. This is the expected behavior of an Executive in a threat situation.

Deconstructing the Strategy

First Phase

The first-phase CEO's basic direction was *accept the government's import tax reduction policy but protect Epsilon.* The distinctive path had three essential thrusts: *reverse Epsilon's public position, move decisively and quickly,* and *take personal responsibility for the reversal.*

Second Phase

The second-phase CEO's basic direction was *remain a large full-service industry association.* There were two essential thrusts: *pursue economies of scale* and *emphasize marketing.*

Classifying the Strategy Content

First Phase

The next step in analysis is to identify the channel of influence used by each essential thrust. The first essential thrust, *reverse the association's public position,* was the primary means by which the accumulating damage to Epsilon was to be terminated. The problem was external, and it was to be addressed by external action: a public announcement of a reversal of position. This mechanism for preventing further damage was rational, not social; it was based on the concept that if you eliminate the source of a problem, the effect should also be eliminated, or at least alleviated. The second thrust was *move decisively and quickly.* There seemed to be a risk that when the CEO revealed Epsilon's position reversal, a spontaneous uprising by many of the association's members would have forced him to recant, and this had to be avoided. The policy reversal itself, therefore, had to be introduced irreversibly and sharply, so it would be in place before resistance could develop. This reasoning relied on a shareholder social channel of influence. The third thrust, *take personal responsibility for the reversal,* was aimed at protecting Epsilon's future by excising the problem; it created a perception that the policy reversal was attached to the first-phase CEO, and then distanced him from the organization. The need to separate the policy reversal from the association itself stemmed mainly from the expectation that lasting, deep resentment would be felt by a large number of Epsilon's members. It was important to move the target of that resentment outside Epsilon so that relations between the association and its members could be healed. The channel of influence, therefore, was shareholder social. In summary the first essential thrust was external rational, while the second and third were shareholder social.

Second Phase

The first essential thrust in the second phase was *pursue economies of scale.* This concept was based on rational economics; it aimed to find a new way to retain a strategic internal resource advantage that Epsilon traditionally had held. Because court-based wage setting would fade away, the strategic importance of the association's labor relations department would gradually decline. The first essential thrust aimed to develop other strategic internal resources to compensate for the labor relations department's expected decrease in importance.[210] That line of thinking is based on an internal rational channel of influence.[211] The second essential thrust was *emphasize marketing.* The intent was to improve Epsilon's power to attract members by improving its external image and visibility.[212] This uses an external social channel. Thus, in the second phase, the first essential thrust's channel of influence was internal rational, and the second's was external social.

Classifying the Strategy Process

First Phase

Each element of strategy must be formed either deliberately or emergently. The first-phase basic direction, *accept the government's import tax reduction policy but protect Epsilon,* came from a specific decision the CEO made whilst engaged in strategic thinking.[213] Therefore, it was deliberate strategy (B1). The three essential thrusts, *reverse the association's public position, move decisively and quickly,* and *take personal responsibility for the reversal,* seem to have been adopted after the basic direction but were all products of the CEO's ongoing strategic thinking, and therefore, were deliberate strategy (C1). [214] The first-phase strategy was entirely deliberate.

Second Phase

The second-phase basic direction, *remain a large full-service industry association,* stemmed from a conscious strategic decision; the CEO said in his interview that he was only interested in working for Epsilon if it followed that direction. He explained in rational terms why and when he adopted it, so it was deliberate strategy (B1).[215] The two essential thrusts, *pursue economies of scale,* [216] and *emphasize marketing,*[217] arose from an ongoing period of strategic thinking and, therefore, were deliberate strategy from Process C1.

SUMMARY

The first-phase CEO allowed a debacle to develop during his stewardship of Epsilon; the strong, closely-aligned views of the majority of the association's members and its most powerful employees combined to distract him from strategic thinking. However, he ultimately recognized his mistake and behaved courageously to limit the long-term damage to his organization.

In the second phase, when both of Epsilon's scale-sensitive core service offerings (labor relations and government relations) began an inexorable decline in strategic relevance, an innovative strategist might have discarded the existing business model and thought about what significant new role the organization could now play. However, as an adaptive strategist, the second-phase CEO decided that the existing business model must be preserved and, therefore, his organization had to be a full-service industry association. From there he addressed the narrower question of what services he could introduce and what marketing techniques he could adopt to make this possible.

The case demonstrates that a sense of scale must be attached to the concept of discontinuous change. Strongly adaptive strategists would have had to operate a long way outside their preferred zone to accept the second-phase CEO's strategic solution for Epsilon, since it involved changing both the internal structure, and the relative power of the major internal staff groups. Strongly innovative strategists would not have accepted the conceptual restrictions that prevented him from discarding his business model and redesigning the concept of the organization around the future market's demand structure.

In a situation such as Epsilon faced, a board has a considerable challenge when appointing a CEO. Only time will tell just how radical an approach is appropriate, but an appointment decision has to made in the present before this information is available.

NOTES

204. The following statement is part of the original case study report: (Epsilon's) CEO sees himself as the steward of a venerable institution.

 CEO: We've been an organization that's always been able to get a continuity of people at the top. Twenty-five people—the top twenty-five people—have three hundred and seventy-nine years' experience with the organization…gives you a heft, a continuity, an experience.

205. CEO: We work very hard to train our own, very rarely do we bring in people from outside to senior posts—very rarely. And it's been a hallmark of the organization, the experience we've got.

206. CEO: Very important strategic issue in this, much debated—I claim as much ownership of it I guess as anyone—was the debate about whether or not as an organization you are a representative body or you provide fee-for-service… And I still hold the view. I'm only interested in working for (Epsilon) on the basis that we are a representative body.

 CEO: And membership gives you a flow of revenue to enable you to retain professional high quality staff.

207. CEO: And I watched (a rival association) decide to give membership away, and it's a fierce competitor in New South Wales. Giving it away and trying to on-sell—taking a full-page ad in (a national newspaper), "Come to our fee-for-service lawyer." They lost $52 million over the last three years.

 CEO: We have to fight every year for every thing in the budget to balance our budget, which we've done always, every year. And I think that made us a bit leaner and meaner and more aggressive…and more hands-on. And I think that's been important. We haven't had a lot of money to throw at things. And it's been a strength rather than a weakness.

208. Deputy CEO: (The CEO) has a much more interesting process and he was determined to bring a lot of the internal processes of the organization up to speed, and things like proper performance appraisal, trying to get

better financial reporting, all those sorts of issues interested (the CEO). And under him we had the first corporate plan I'd ever seen for the organization.

209. CEO: And simple philosophy, but that's what would underpin it, get close to your members, be their voice, sell that, on not too many things, not all things, half a dozen important areas of activity. And that was what our three year plan set out to do, and we're basically sticking to it. We're now writing another three-year plan.

    Deputy CEO: But (the CEO) has really modernized a lot of the thinking, with the thinking, the corporate planning processes—for all staff to say well what are we doing, how relevant is it, should we be thinking about new things? So someone can say well I've got an idea, I think there's so much demand for this, let's have a look at this. And then you start to forge a new service under that.

210. This approach was succeeding at the time of the case study.

    Deputy CEO: When we do surveys of our members on what service is very important, (labor relations) was ninety-five (percent), and economics was ninety-three, and the rest were way behind. Some were fifteen, like environment.

211. It relies on the concepts of Resource-Based View literature (Teece et al. 1997).

212. Deputy CEO: I think we need a high public profile for our organization because we don't deal with all our members every day and they need to see us through free branding. Brand can be very powerful, because that makes our members feel, well, they're out there fighting for them, they're out there advocating their interests, and they're just out there, and isn't it good that the organization is a powerful player. So that's all positioning—ideas around that strong brand that we have to have as an association.

213. Interviewer: Now what brought that on? That was a strategic decision. What drove that decision?

    Deputy CEO: It was driven by - I used to raise it with (the previous CEO) that I thought that the companies that were holding us back from making the decision, weren't the ones that were going to take the organization forward. And that the new emerging companies – (import taxes) weren't that relevant to them. And so I said we have to hitch our sail to the winners, and try and build a competitive industry.

    Deputy CEO: And I remember it was in late January, and (the previous CEO) was down the coast, and I rang him up. And (one of our directors) said "Good luck, hitting your head against this wall". So I rang (the previous CEO)... And on that phone call, he changed his mind.

214. CEO: I've to give credit here to (the previous CEO), doing an about face on our policy. We talked about it, but he came to the decision that we're on the wrong (path). And he got some input from various people about that. And it was being debated in the public arena anyway, but he could see that we were on the wrong path of arguing for protection (against imports). And it took his leadership to take that to the policy body to say that we've got to move away from this position.

Interviewer: And that would have been for a combination of theoretical and pragmatic reasons, partly to do with recognizing reality, and partly to do with recognizing some economic principles?

CEO: Recognizing suddenly that some of our biggest Australian manufacturers were moving their production into China for the first time, and Vietnam. Those frontiers were opening. And suddenly some were saying "Well, not too sure whether you're right here, you know, we're earning now; big parts of our components are starting to come in, we've just put our (major product component) into South East Asia, and we're not too sure we want those (import taxes) as high as they were because of the impact on our cost." So it came about as industry started to engage and (the previous CEO) got the title of One Hundred and Eighty Degree Man. He did a flip. He made a very important speech, a lecture, Kingsley Laffer speech at Sydney University where he staked out the new territory and it coincided with the views of most of the people sitting around our board table that was the right way to go.

215. CEO: Very important strategic issue in this, much debated—I claim as much ownership of it I guess as anyone—was the debate about whether or not as an organization you are a representative body or you provide fee-for-service. Do you say to a company, "You are a member of this organization, we're going to represent your interests" and, therefore, the collective interests, and we're not so—you don't get a tangible product out of that, that it's important to have a voice to government, in the media, in the community, influencing legislation, influencing opinion. And I absolutely steadfastly believe that's the core. So I watched all the other organizations try and bolster their revenue, increasingly move to a model where they brought down their membership subscriptions, almost gave membership away, to try and on-sell fee-for-service. And to me that just cast them into the mould of a consulting firm, and when you do fee-for-service to one company, you're loyal to that company, and the interests of the rest could be prejudiced. Who knows? And it took you in a different mindset. And I still hold the view. I'm only interested in working for (Epsilon) on the basis that we are a representative body.

216. Deputy CEO: (The previous CEO) retired, (the present CEO) took over. (This CEO) had—his real drive was with the members, particularly in (the

Australian state of) Victoria. He's good at marketing, gets out there, he spent a lot of time, and he had a lot of success in supporting membership and driving membership. And that was a great strength. But he came in from a different perspective. He had a long history in (labor relations) areas, and whatever, but that marketing, getting out there, selling membership was one of his really major issues. When (his predecessor) retired he came in, and I think he sought to bring a culture of business development, membership development, growth. It was very much the hallmark of (the CEO's) vision for the organization. (The previous CEO) had been much more about power, and influence, and us being seen very much to be part of the scene. And we had no problems with membership in fact under the former vision, it seemed to come, we'd just get it from a different direction. But that was the division that was to mark a turning point in terms of the strategy of the organization. So (this CEO) came in, he saw the potential; he was Victorian-based so he had a pretty good knowledge here. And ...I think, the possibility of the merger got in his nostrils and then his vision started to form more generally about the direction he saw the organization going in...

217. Interviewer: Now the concept of maybe strengthening the brand or broadening the brand, going from being a sort of (labor relations) player to being a broad player, did that come from a person or process? How did it happen?

Deputy CEO: I was given a lot of encouragement in the early days to do more—when (the CEO) took over and we did the merger.

8
Theta

Theta was the Australian subsidiary of an overseas component manufacturing company. This meant that it received its policy directives—in effect, updates and interpretations of its underlying purpose—from parent-company executives who effectively (though not literally) were Theta's board or shareholders. Theta's strategic constraints were otherwise generally similar to those of other Australian component manufacturers.

HISTORY

Australia's automobile industry developed under the protection of high taxes on imported cars, and restrictions on imports of their components. Theta's parent, a European second tier automobile component manufacturer, saw an opportunity to benefit from these restrictions by setting up a manufacturing operation in Australia to supply similar components directly to the local market. That operation, Theta, was successful for many years until a major change occurred. From 1984, the Australian federal government began to reduce the local auto industry's protection against imports. This change in public policy gradually increased the level of competition from imported cars, and from imported components for locally-made cars. Theta was a medium-sized organization with five hundred employees.

THE FIRST PHASE: A FREE HAND IN A SMALL MARKET

In 1960, an employee of a European automobile component manufacturer was given the job of carrying out a feasibility study on setting up a manufacturing subsidiary in Australia. The concept was to function as a second tier Australian manufacturer, by supplying original equipment components to local first tier auto companies. His assessment was positive, and he volunteered to establish the new firm himself as founding CEO. His strategic assessment was similar to that of the existing Australian auto component makers. He saw that the market was too small for economically-viable local manufacture of cars, so the auto and component industries were totally reliant on the government protecting them against imports. In this type of low-volume manufacturing, economies of scale improve very rapidly with increased production volume. This meant that profitability would be heavily dependent on volume—whoever made the largest number of each component would have the lowest cost, resulting in a profitable and dominant position. By far, the biggest market for components was supplying them to the local auto manufacturers as original equipment. Therefore, Theta's strategy was centered on maximizing these sales. This implied two specific requirements. First, component prices in Australia had to remain higher than international prices, so all necessary means had to be used to ensure that Australian car manufacturers continued to be forced by the federal government to use locally-made components. Second, it was essential to prevent new entrants from manufacturing Theta's type of components in Australia, because this could fragment the market and spoil Theta's economies of scale.

The founding CEO established Theta successfully and after two years, the parent company invited him to extend his tour of duty in Australia. Consistent with his rather adventurous and innovative inclinations, he said he would stay "as long as there is always something new and exciting." Within a few years, he established a small subsidiary in New Zealand and eventually followed it with a number of other small operations in Asia. Meanwhile, for nearly forty years, he adhered to his original strategy for profitable auto component manufacturing in Australia.

The first phase ended soon after 2000. By then, Theta's long-established strategy had finally become unworkable because the

Australian government's auto industry protection scheme had largely been dismantled. Local content requirements had been discontinued. Import taxes had decreased greatly and it was government policy to reduce them to negligible levels. Theta's share of the local original equipment component market had declined due to increased use of imported components. Meanwhile the share of the local automobile market held by imported cars had increased from 20 percent to over 50 percent, so sales of locally made cars had decreased. This meant that Theta's sales of original equipment components for locally made cars were being squeezed in two ways—the company had a shrinking share of a shrinking market.

THE SECOND PHASE: RESTRUCTURE

Given Theta's deteriorating business situation, a change of strategy was inevitable. In practice, it was precipitated when a different parent company executive became responsible for the Australian operation. He appointed a new CEO to replace Theta's founding CEO, who had reached retirement age, and he also established a strong "fix it or close it" policy, defining "fix it" as obtaining sufficient sales volume and price to make Theta satisfactorily profitable. At the same time, the Asian subsidiaries that the founding CEO had established were transferred to the management control of various head office executives in Europe. Theta continued to provide support services for them through its existing structure, but had no command over them. This narrowed the new CEO's range of strategic options, by preventing him from viewing Theta and the Asian subsidiaries as a total operation and seeking overall synergies.

The new CEO accepted that head office would not change the fix-it-or-close-it policy directive, so his task was to implement it. His first move was conceptual; he decided to regard Theta as consisting of several separable business streams. After analyzing the data, he identified three streams: manufacturing and original equipment sales, aftermarket and specialized sales, and the service group supporting the Asian subsidiaries now directed by the parent company. Seeing no substantial synergies between these streams, the CEO decided to treat them as individual divisions; if one or more had to close down, the others could continue.

He made a detailed financial analysis of the largest division—manufacturing and original equipment sales—to find out what it would take to make it viable. He concluded that it needed to win all of the new original equipment contracts offered by all of the local auto manufacturers in the following five years. At that time, one of Theta's two main types of product held one third of the local original-equipment market, and the other main product type, two thirds. The CEO met with each of the local auto companies individually to find out why Theta was losing market share, and they all told him they were dissatisfied with the service his firm provided. This reinforced his view that the division would require changes in its practices and performance to regain viability. He emphasized to the divisional executive team that they had to win every significant contract or their division would close down.

An independent distributor importing the parent company's standard products could probably have achieved the aftermarket and specialized sales division's existing functions. To be viable, the division needed to offer some special advantage over a distributor. The CEO set up a brainstorming team to look for solutions, and a significant new opportunity to add value was found. Theta's sales to the Australian mining industry could be expanded by introducing purpose-designed mining products. A Theta study center, based on a team of engineers transferred from the manufacturing and original equipment division, could work with the mining industry to identify product concepts for detailed development by the parent company's engineers. After development these would become new global products made by the parent company. It was reasonable to locate the study center in Australia because of its large mining sector.

The remaining division had until this point managed the Asian subsidiaries. Henceforth, it would just provide support services, with most of the important management decisions coming from head office. Generally, this division was already operating in the way head office required.

ANALYSIS

Classifying the First-Phase Strategist

The first analytical step is to classify the strategists' cognitive biases under the typology developed in Chapter 2. In Theta's case, there were different CEOs in the first and second phases and each had acted as the firm's strategist, so two separate analyses are required. This section concerns the first-phase strategist: the founding CEO.

Change-Readiness

There are several indications of the founding CEO's change-readiness. First, and completely contrary to head office's expectation, after making a feasibility study in Australia he volunteered to return personally and set up the new manufacturing subsidiary—something well outside his previous experience.[218] Second, after completing that mission and being asked to stay on and run the Australian subsidiary, he indicated he would do so as long as there was "always something new and exciting."[219] Third, he subsequently persuaded his head office to allow him to create a series of additional subsidiaries in various countries.[220] These events indicate that he seems to have been attracted to discontinuous change, and had an aversion to the absence of change. This is the profile of an innovator.

Cognitive Emphasis

To identify the founding CEO's cognitive emphasis we need to find his strategic imperative—what over-riding consideration drove his business decisions? His strategy and much of his general approach were the same as for most other second tier Australian auto component firms, so his most distinctive activity was starting new subsidiaries in the Asia Pacific region. The process for doing this involved negotiating with various Asian governments, making command decisions on whether to go ahead with new firms, and personally overseeing the growing portfolio of firms that resulted. The firms in the portfolio were small, and were heavily protected by the Asian governments. None of them seemed likely to create major profits or public benefits in the short term, though they had prospects of doing so eventually. However, the whole program did do one positive thing immediately: it let him engage in high-level negotiations and make powerful decisions. His behavior, therefore, seems consistent with an egotistic cognitive emphasis.

Cognitive Bias

Putting the change-readiness and cognitive emphasis together, the founding CEO is classified as an innovative egotist, or Entrepreneur. The term suits him well. He was driven by a need to find or create new challenges, and these took the form of new business ventures—first Theta itself, and then a series of other subsidiary operations. Unlike the Entrepreneurs in the Alpha and Gamma cases, his circumstances did not permit him to design his main organization to suit his personality, so he added extraneous activities that suited his personality.

Classifying the Second-Phase Strategist

When he took control of Theta, the second-phase CEO addressed the job in a markedly different way from his predecessor, indicating a different cognitive bias.

Change-Readiness

The new CEO provided clues to his change-readiness in four areas. First, when he took office and needed to fill gaps in his own plans, he assembled a brainstorming group.[221] Brainstorming is a technique that simulates an innovation preference,[222] so it would probably be used mainly by adaptors. Second, his approach to solving the strategic problem was highly methodical and step-by-step rather than vision-driven.[223] Third, he showed no dislike of detail, and impulsiveness seems to have been notably absent.[224] Fourth, he accepted his instructions from head office without objecting to them, and followed them precisely.[225] This looks like a portrait of an adaptor.

Cognitive Emphasis

The primacy of materialism in the new CEO's motivation is evident in his choices. If he had emphasized egotism he would probably have tried to change or subvert the brief he was given—it inevitably gave him little decision-making power, and to other people it must have looked as if he had accepted an unglamorous assignment. If he had been driven by altruism he might also have resisted the brief, because it forced him to allow materialistic considerations to determine whether employment would be destroyed. As a materialist, however, he regarded his assignment as a tough and unpleasant job, but a necessary one. He proceeded to do it by making a financial analysis and using the results to set objective, materialistic survival criteria. These criteria would control the outcome more-or-less automatically rather than requiring him to exercise arbitrary decision-making power, as an egotist might have preferred. His approach did not create special advantages either for employees or other people, as an altruist might have preferred.

Cognitive Bias

The above analysis has identified the new CEO as an adaptive materialist, the type labeled Executive in Chapter 2. Members of this group tend to form strategy only when it has become clear that tactical solutions will not succeed. They like to subdivide their major decisions where possible and prefer to defer each part until maximum clarity is achieved. In this case, the situation was serious and the parent company's policy directive insisted on urgent action, so a strategic rather than a tactical solution was adopted, but the chosen solution deferred any strong, irreversible action for up to five years, during which it could be hoped that greater clarity or additional options might be found. The quality of results Executives achieve is typically determined by their executive ability rather than their imagination. The new CEO's behavior was consistent with this profile.

Deconstructing the Strategy

First Phase

The founding CEO was starting a new firm. His employer dictated an underlying purpose, and allowed him to propose his own strategy to satisfy it. His crucial concern was the small size of the Australian automotive component market, which necessitated three things: high levels of protection against imports, near-monopoly production volumes of each type of component, and a focus on supplying original equipment to the auto companies. That is, his basic direction was to *maximize protected original equipment component sales.* The broad path had two essential thrusts: *ensure that government protection is sustained* to guarantee that the Australian market for his component range was satisfied by local production, and *pre-empt competitive entry* by other component manufacturers in the same field, who might otherwise have set up factories in Australia and fragmented the market.

Second Phase

Theta's second-phase basic direction was *restructure to maximize future survival and earnings prospects.* The broad path had three essential thrusts. First, the CEO would *divide Theta into three independent divisions*; that is, make manufacturing/original equipment, aftermarket/specialized, and overseas services into separate businesses, any of which could potentially survive the closure of one or both of the other two. Second, he would *use financial modeling* to set and enforce viability criteria for the manufacturing division. Third, he would *create a center of mining expertise* to make the aftermarket division potentially viable.

Classifying the Strategy Content

First Phase

We classify strategy content by identifying the channel of influence that each essential thrust relied on to achieve its intended purpose. Both of the first-phase essential thrusts, *ensure that government protection is sustained* and *pre-empt competitive entry,* aimed to influence external people's decisions through rule-bound (and therefore rational) external game-playing processes.[226] The channel for both thrusts was, therefore, external rational.

Second Phase

The intention of the first essential thrust, *divide Theta into three independent divisions,* was to eliminate cross-subsidies between various parts of Theta, and the chosen method was to separate the business streams, giving visibility to the financial performance of each as a stand-alone entity. This was an example of applying rational economic forces internally, so the channel was internal rational. The aim of the second thrust, *use financial modeling,* was to minimize the influence of internal social arguments on how the manufacturing division was managed during its critical reform period. The CEO's technique was to impose economic rationality on the internal reforms and on the final decision criteria. This means the second thrust was internal rational. *Create a center of mining expertise* was an attempt to create a successful additional business activity to help make the aftermarket division viable. The intention was to improve Theta's internal resource endowment by adding a capability that would be relatively difficult for others to replicate.[227] This implies an internal rational channel. Thus, all three essential thrusts were internal rational.

Classifying the Strategy Process

First Phase

Next, we classify the process that produced each element of the strategy, by using the process model shown in Figure 1. The basic direction for Theta in the first phase, *maximize protected original equipment component sales,* must have been adopted either deliberately (B1) in a conscious strategic decision or emergently (B2) without a strategic decision being made. It is clear that the founding CEO consciously worked out his strategy during the feasibility study he made (B1). Since the basic direction was deliberate, each essential thrust could have been adopted either deliberately (C1), or emergently (C2). Both thrusts (*ensure that government protection is sustained* and *pre-empt competitive entry*) were adopted deliberately (C1) as outcomes of the feasibility study. Thus, the entire first-phase strategy was deliberate.

Second Phase

The second-phase basic direction, *restructure to maximize future survival and earnings prospects,* was part of the new CEO's solution to the strategy problem. Because it resulted from conscious strategic thinking (B1), it was deliberate strategy. The first two essential thrusts, *divide Theta into three independent divisions* and *use financial modeling,* resulted from two related, conscious strategic decisions (C1). Both were made by the new CEO soon after his appointment, and were aimed at overcoming Theta's financial challenges. The first decision was to break the organization up into divisions, one of which (the manufacturing division) was known to be the main source of Theta's poor performance. The second decision was to set financial survival criteria for the troubled division. The third thrust, *create a center of mining expertise,* also came from a strategic thinking process (C1), but it was quite different from the process the new CEO used in his initial analysis. After completing the initial analysis, he selected a group of his staff to brainstorm solutions to the problems he had not solved on his own, and during fairly unstructured discussion the center of expertise concept seemed to arise serendipitously.[228] The brainstorming process was intended to be more tactical than strategic, but it appears that a member of the group took the opportunity to engage in strategic thinking, and proposed an essential thrust. The new CEO then made a strategic decision to adopt the proposal. Because the outcome was a deliberate strategic decision, the third essential thrust was deliberate strategy. In summary, all elements of the second-phase strategy were deliberate.

SUMMARY

In the first phase, an Entrepreneur was appointed to found an Australian manufacturing subsidiary for an existing European company, and he did this successfully. His employer then offered him an indefinite extension of his appointment as CEO of the subsidiary, and he accepted this for "as long as there is always something new and exciting." Looking at this proviso, which is very consistent with the distinctions between adaptors and innovators summarized in Appendix 1, we might ask why an Entrepreneur stayed and managed a simple, almost static, defensive strategic situation for a period of nearly forty years, when the assignment obviously did not match his cognitive bias. I put this question to him in his interview and he attributed his decision to "sheer greed."[229]

When the Entrepreneur's long-established strategy at Theta eventually became untenable, the head office appointed an Executive as CEO with the mission of putting the company into survival mode and dismantling it if necessary. The Executive approached this task methodically and efficiently, laying the groundwork for an orderly outcome without prejudging what it would be.

NOTES

218. Founding CEO: And then we went back, made a recommendation that we should have an engagement in Australia, and then there was this big meeting presided over by (the parent's CEO) and his last summing up words I recall were, "Well, it really seems a good idea to go and do this but I don't think we can because we've got nobody to run it." And that was when I piped up and said "Oh yes you do." And I hate to remember the look I got. I started fearing for my future. So nothing further happened for another week, and then I had to present myself to the boss, was asked was I serious about it, and was I prepared to do this. And (because I had never) built a factory offshore, I had all the confidence in the world. And I did it, and so

it started. And I must say that (the parent company in Europe) used to run these things on the basis of an extremely long leash.

219. Founding CEO: It's probably been the longest two years in my life. And when that came up for discussion, I had a discussion with my chairman, and when he asked me did I want to extend it...I'll be happy to stay on as long as there is always something new and exciting... And we agreed on that. That was as simple as that.

220. Founding CEO: I think my main intention at the time was to (first make) the company grow, having made the decision to go into Australia. And then beyond that to grow and start something new somewhere else. That was the main motivation. After that came the question "Where?" and "How?" And the only way that you can find that out is by going around talking to people and playing the famous Caliphate of Baghdad that sits back and listens most of the time.

221. CEO: We were looking at ways of increasing our aftermarket business, so we said "What can we do to grow this? Sure we can grow it at the growth rates we're experiencing, but we can look outside that—in a sense a specialization." And it came out of a brainstorming discussion on how we can grow the business and where we can see an opportunity.

CEO: We'd take people from different parts of the organization into a brainstorming team. And we might for example have a sales manager, who's out there in the marketplace seeing new product and seeing customer reaction. We would obviously have the head of marketing, we have the product development person. Also in that case I'd drag somebody out of design and development.

Interviewer: So this would be something that you've decided to do, and then you'd decide who to have there?

CEO: Yes.

222. (Kirton 2003 p. 171).

223. CEO: (W)hen I assumed the responsibilities at (Theta) we sat down and did an analysis of what was an unfavorable situation at the time, and initially we identified the most critical survival issues. So a lot of the strategies that have driven us over the past two years have effectively been survival strategies, not growth strategies. And we identified two or three key elements and effectively put the bulk of our resources into addressing those.

224. CEO: It was done by bringing the senior executive group together and conducting a formal review. We were looking at the performance and the budgets, the figures, forward business plan. And reviewed the issues. But in doing that, we then looked effectively at (Strengths, Weaknesses,

Opportunities and Threats) analysis. With more focus on the weakness than the opportunities.

225. CEO: My view was to add value, to add value to the global organization because I was not going to change the restructuring that was occurring in (Europe) and the shift to global product lines, global thinking centered out of (global headquarters)—that was not going to be changed by (Theta), or (the Asia Pacific regional office). So my approach to that was to be the best service provider I could, to have relevance as a service provider, and also to provide a little bit of strategic thinking where it was lacking in terms of those product lines. But not to be as dominant in terms of the strategic thinking as we had been at the stage when (Europe) didn't know what was happening.

Interviewer: Because you think they've decided to weigh in, and you're not going to stop them.

CEO: Precisely, and not only have they decided, they've seen the importance in terms of their global future of being part of Asia. Not all, but more and more. More and more. Every meeting I go to over there, there are more converts.

226. With regard to the first thrust, I suggest that lobbying government as a way to influence public policy is a rule-bound game-playing process in most developed countries. It was especially so in Australia during the period of economic reform that began in 1984. The second thrust was another game-playing process; possible new entrants were to be outmaneuvered to keep them out of the market.

227. CEO: We've persuaded the head office that we should establish a center of excellence here in Australia for mining, and there we're starting with almost a blank sheet of paper, to build up a mining business, which ultimately we will see as a global business.

Interviewer: What drove that?

CEO: (The) fact that we saw an opportunity, that the knowledge that we acquired of the mining business through being involved with it through our aftermarket business, revealed to us that it was not well structured, that it was a very fragmented industry in terms of (Theta's core technology). There were a lot of small players, few of them had the technology and the resources that we had available in Australia as well as globally, and they certainly didn't have access to the Research and Development that we have access to both in Australia and through the (parent's) global R and D facilities. So we saw that as a gap in the marketplace.

228. Interviewer: The process there is of interest, because it looks on the face of it like a major creative spark, and I'd like to know something about the

anatomy of that. Of how you go from "Let's brainstorm about product opportunities," to "Hey, here's one."

CEO: It's interesting if we take that example. We were brainstorming a product, which then progressed, and we were dealing with some of the commercialization and miniaturization issues of some of the features we needed for that product. And that led us to think that this product has an application for mining, and that led us, and in fact our managing director from New Zealand was part of that process as well, because we were talking with him, and that then led him to think of other perhaps mining applications, and that then led us to the whole center of excellence of mining.

229. Founding CEO: Well I guess I can only speak now from personal experience, and I think it was nothing but sheer greed.

9
Kappa

Kappa was an Australian company with a government-backed monopoly over exporting a specific locally-produced commodity. The existence of that monopoly was the source of most of the complexity in Kappa's strategic situation. Essentially, the political and economic issues brought into play by granting this privilege to a profit-oriented, stock-exchange-listed company caused such complexity in the external environment that there was no feasible strategic solution. Ingenuity and determination produced a partial solution.

HISTORY

Many years ago, most of the Australian producers of a certain commodity believed that various overseas buyers and sellers of the commodity had market power. They thought their best strategy in this situation was for all of the Australian exports to be pooled and handled by a single seller, thus giving that seller market power also. Because they were concerned about the possibility of opportunistic free-riding by individual local producers, they demanded that the Australian federal government grant the single seller a legal monopoly. The government yielded to their political pressure and set up a special government body to export the commodity. That arrangement satisfied the producers for decades, but in a period of zealous economic reform commencing in the 1980s, economists argued that commodity-dealing was a commercial activity, not an administrative one, and, therefore, was unsuitable for governments. However, the politically-powerful producers wanted the monopoly to remain in force. A partial solution would have been to convert the existing government body into a producers' cooperative association that retained the monopoly subject to government regulation and oversight. This approach was unacceptable to the economic reformers, who anticipated that a producers' cooperative association with thousands of members would lack efficiency and dynamism. In their view, the new organization had to be a stock-exchange-listed company. That immediately created a major difficulty—if the shares in a company could be traded, over time many of them would change hands. This implied that the company would eventually not be controlled by producers, but it would continue to hold a monopoly, thus putting the producers into a captive situation. The chosen solution was to set up a complex mechanism involving not only regulators, but also a bipartite board of directors made up of separate groups representing producers and investors. The producers, whose shares were not to be traded publicly, would always elect a majority of the board members including the chairperson. The ordinary investors would elect the balance of the board. This concept was implemented, producing an inherently-divided board and an incoherent underlying purpose requiring Kappa to maximize returns both to producers and to the firm itself.

The producers viewed the new structure with considerable suspicion, an attitude that was soon reinforced by two developments. First, when Kappa became a company, the service the producers received from it quickly deteriorated from its historic standard. This suggested that they were going to be treated as captive suppliers. Second, indications and rumors emerged from Kappa suggesting that an entrepreneurial trading mentality was developing there, rather than the traditional focus on maximizing the income received simply by selling the product on behalf of the producers. The producers did not necessarily object to Kappa selling in advance of production when prices were high, or holding product in stock when prices were low, or taking similar modest steps to stabilize the market and maximize producers' income, but an outright speculative trading approach could lead to risky activity. This might be attractive to stock market investors, but it was an appalling prospect as far as producers were concerned. When they observed these developments, the producers became stridently dissatisfied, and Kappa's board responded by appointing a new CEO in 2000. Kappa was a medium-sized company with six hundred employees.

THE FIRST PHASE: GETTING ON COURSE QUICKLY

As usual, the Kappa case will be addressed in two phases. The first phase covers the new CEO's first months in office, beginning late in 2000. The second phase begins after his first intensive program of meetings with producers, and ends with the case study interviews in 2002 to 2003.

By the time the new CEO took office, he had an idea what had caused the trends that had alarmed the producers. He immediately focused on calming producers and dealing with those causes. This dominated his first-phase strategy. He addressed the problem by taking two initiatives. The first was to meet with groups of producers in various key towns, assuring them of three things: he understood that they had the ultimate power in Kappa, he understood that they were aggrieved, and he regarded their concerns as valid. While this shareholder relations initiative was proceeding, he gave the remainder of his attention to his second initiative: implementing the promises he was making to the producers. He interviewed Kappa's top fifty managers individually, and concluded that his initial diagnosis was correct. The top management team was not providing the basic leadership needed to ensure coherence in the organization, and this had allowed what he regarded as wild behavior to emerge at lower levels. His solution was to reassign or replace almost all of the top team. This established his authority in the company, which helped him in the second phase.

THE SECOND PHASE: SUSTAINABLE STRATEGIC CONCEPTS

Producers and potential stock-market investors wanted to know how Kappa would address the problems that flowed from its bipartite ownership structure. Because the CEO had no way to alleviate the highest-level problem—the divided board—he could only try to minimize its adverse consequences. Accordingly, his strategic objective in the second phase was to achieve a viable underlying purpose for the firm. He believed this could largely be achieved by adopting a business model that suited Kappa's circumstances. The company's constitution stated that it must maximize net returns to producers, but did not state how this was to be accomplished. As far as the CEO was concerned, the export monopoly was not the main strategic issue; Kappa had to be configured so that it could be successful whether or not the monopoly continued in the long term. The model he introduced and enforced stated that Kappa was a paid asset manager. In effect, the firm's role in the commodity market was to deal with the managed assets in the explicit interests of the assets' owners, the producers. This departed from the historical view that Kappa was a value-added marketer with a focus on the buyer of the product, but it also rejected the concept of outright speculation.

ANALYSIS

Classifying the Strategist

The CEO did not have either the time or the inclination to engage in extensive high-level tactical thinking, so in the second phase he engaged an outside consultant to work with him personally.[230] The consultant was probably the source of most of the high-level tactics adopted in the second phase, including the paid-asset-manager concept. However, he worked in support of a strategic agenda set by the CEO, who was happy to have an idea person to propose specific implementation solutions. The CEO was clearly the strategist.

Change-Readiness

The CEO's emphasis was on understanding the issues in individual detail.[231] Rather than having an overall vision, he preferred to work step by step to generate a workable solution, implementing each section of the solution individually and sequentially.[232] This step-by-step, problem-solving approach is characteristic of an adaptor.

Cognitive Emphasis

The CEO made it clear in his interview that the producers were the primary stakeholders in Kappa, but they were not the only group the organization served.[233] Once the business model was in place, it appeared that his practice was to give primary consideration to advancing Kappa's own commercial interests.[234] That led him to rely on the business model to satisfy the producers, while he worked to maximize returns to Kappa—an approach that suggests that he was a materialist. An egotist might have preferred to satisfy both producers and investors whilst maximizing the CEO's power to act arbitrarily and unilaterally. An altruist might have preferred to satisfy investors whilst maximizing benefits to some other party—probably producers, but perhaps some non-stakeholder group. The CEO, therefore, fit a materialist model well, and did not fit egotist or altruist models.

Cognitive Bias

The CEO emerges from the preceding analysis as an adaptive materialist, or Executive. This description seems to fit his emphasis on solving problems carefully, and improving the firm one step at a time without challenging the most important of the externally imposed limitations.

Deconstructing the Strategy

First Phase

The first-phase basic direction was *address the key problems urgently.* The broad path had two essential thrusts: *assure the producers that their needs are Kappa's primary concern,* and *achieve internal coherence.*

Second Phase

In the second phase, the basic direction was *place Kappa on a sound business footing.* Kappa's initial lack of soundness as a business seems to have been mainly a result of policy problems; due to externally-imposed requirements, the firm had a bipartite board that was ineffectual, and an underlying purpose that was incoherent. The basic direction was the CEO's attempt to use strategy to alleviate the incoherence of the underlying purpose. The broad path consisted of one essential thrust: *create a viable business model.*

Classifying the Strategy Content

First Phase

The essential thrusts of any strategy have to rely on channels of influence if they are to take effect. Identifying these channels is one of the analytical steps that are necessary before a strategy can be understood. In the first phase, the first essential thrust, *assure the producers that their needs are Kappa's primary concern,* was aimed at alleviating the key stakeholders' dissatisfaction in the short term by improving communication with them. The producers were Kappa's dominant shareholders—collectively they controlled Kappa's board. The intention of the first thrust was to address a social problem (the producers' frustration) by using a social measure (improved communication). Hence, the channel of influence for the thrust was shareholder social. The CEO adopted the second essential thrust, *achieve internal coherence,* because he believed that the issues that were frustrating the producers would not have arisen and would not continue, if the organization were internally coherent. An inadequately directed staff was annoying Kappa's dominant shareholders, and this had to be stopped by asserting more effective social control over Kappa's internal human resources. This, therefore, used an internal social channel of influence. In summary, the first essential thrust was shareholder social, and the second was internal social.

Second Phase

There was only one essential thrust in the second phase: *create a viable business model.* The purpose of the business model was to establish an ongoing process to guide and restrict Kappa's business approach: that is, to provide a functional proxy for a coherent underlying purpose. The CEO had identified a crucial function that was not being performed by the ineffectual board. He found a solution that was potentially acceptable to both sides of the board, and negotiated with the parties, persuading them to accept it. The solution cannot be considered totally rational since it left the basic problem (a divided, ineffectual board) in place; it was a social compromise. The channel of influence was shareholder social.

Classifying the Strategy Process

First Phase

As explained in Chapter 3, each element of the strategy must have formed either deliberately or emergently. The first-phase basic direction was *address the key problems urgently.* In his interview, the CEO indicated that he adopted this direction deliberately (B1).[235] The two essential thrusts, *assure the producers that their needs are Kappa's primary concern* and *achieve internal coherence,* were also adopted consciously by the CEO (C1) so they were both deliberate strategy.[236] Therefore, all elements of the first-phase strategy were deliberate.

Second Phase

The second-phase basic direction was *place Kappa on a sound business footing.* This direction came from a deliberate decision (B1).[237] It was a second-round outcome of the CEO's first-phase strategic thinking; the item achieved primary importance in the second phase. The essential thrust, *create a viable business model,* was adopted deliberately by the CEO in a strategic decision, so once again it was deliberate strategy (C1).[238] The entire second-phase strategy was deliberate.

SUMMARY

Kappa's CEO was appointed in the context of conflicting environmental forces; there was no feasible solution zone. The "paid asset manager" concept helped to limit the effects of the inherent conflict between the interests of the producers, the private investors, and the Australian government—but it was a partial solution resting on all three parties making potentially-unstable compromises. First, the producers had to accept the disadvantages of converting Kappa from a captive servant into a contracted agent motivated to maximize the fees it could charge. Second, the stock market had to accept that Kappa could only keep its valuable export monopoly—and, therefore, its market power—if it accepted a business model that substantially constrained the firm's use of its market power to make profits. Third, the government had to accept that an inherently unstable solution was better than an immediate political problem of some magnitude.

In the case study period, Kappa could only hope to thrive under this solution if it made two immediate, fundamental changes in its approach. First, it had to deliver the contracted services to the producers efficiently and attentively, in place of an emerging tendency to regard the producers as captive suppliers. Second, it had to focus on becoming a paid asset manager rather than a free-wheeling entrepreneurial trader, which the CEO and his consultant both saw as an emerging trend prior to his appointment.[239] These were major changes; they constituted an upheaval in Kappa's emerging culture.

Deliberately initiating an upheaval, or discontinuous change, is innovative behavior. However to manage that upheaval Kappa's leader had to reform the firm's administrative performance and negotiate a new business model with shareholders, without causing undue disruption. This required sustained attention to detail—an adaptive behavior. No single CEO could have been truly comfortable exercising both of these approaches to change. In practice, Kappa's board selected an adaptor, and he dealt with the situation in adaptive style; he subdivided it and resolved the pieces individually, according to the urgency of each aspect.

NOTES

230. Strategy Consultant: But I think, and in this case certainly, the arrival of (the CEO) was a very important factor because he's very intelligent, he's very energetic, he's mentally tough, and he has a well developed sense of what will work and what will not work. So that's a good start. What I think he didn't have and perhaps didn't have the time, he didn't have the time to do all of the thinking, that he's too busy. So who's going to do the thinking, who's going to do the analytical stuff? And that as it happened fell to a boutique advisory firm, which was the firm that I owned. And so, analytics are the other thing that are fundamental. You can show two people the same piece of information, and say what does it mean, and one person will say "Well it doesn't mean anything," and the other person will say, "My God, Geoff, look at this, this is amazing."

    Interviewer: So to capture the insight you really draw on an eclectic collection of information. What you can get and what you are beginning to think you might need, and the end product is insight.

    SC: The end product is insight, and one of the things I think is fundamental—we are now onto this question of information input—here we sought to think about the industry in terms of archetypes.

231. CEO: Well I say personally, I'm very uncomfortable if I don't understand something. I don't like ignorance; you've got to understand things. Secondly, you've got to be able to influence them, because ultimately you're accountable, responsible for them. So it's an abdication of responsibility, of what people pay you for in my view, if you don't understand and you can't influence. So, sitting on top of a company or an industry or a business that I don't understand, or don't believe I can control, is not a—to some extent—is not a happy thing for me to be involved in. So I operate basically at the level of vision, and detail too, on inquiry, and I challenge people, and I take them to task—in a nice way—but I get to the bottom of things and understand them. So I wouldn't be comfortable, a bit like Warren Buffett, you know, don't invest in something you don't understand. I wouldn't be the CEO of a company I think I didn't understand, or more importantly, couldn't influence, in terms of where it was headed or what it did.

232. CEO: So the values were being clear about capability, understanding what you could do, what you couldn't do, understanding what was feasible given all the constraints, progressively moving to realize that, not panicking, not saying, "Oh God, the (monopoly) is going to go tomorrow, we'll all be doomed," because panic will lead mostly to recklessness and poor decision-making and you'll pay for that in the long run. So really just being very clear about what you have to do to get where you want to go, making sure that was an acceptable view of the future, and then building the capability progressively to realize it and through all that, continuing to refine and test.

233. CEO: You know we've always said from the beginning that our challenge is to find ways of making money for our shareholders that help our (producers) make money and our international customers make money, because they're the only ones that will pay all of us.

234. CEO: When we looked at the export system, we thought of ourselves like a fund manager. Managing a fund—instead of people putting their money into the fund, the (producers) put their (product) into the fund. We turned that (product) into money and gave it back to them. And so we formulated a lot of (plans) about growing the value in that fund, and then paying the manager, which was (Kappa), like a fund manager, so a portion of our income was dependent on the performance of the fund. And again, that was a very sensible way of aligning the interests of the people that were in the fund with the manager. So if we made more money for the fund we'd both benefit.

235. CEO: For example, we used to have a regional structure; (then) they pulled everything into the center, but they didn't have the systems or the

processes to run a business (that way). So basically we had no one out in the (producing areas) servicing the (producers). And as well as poor service, that was one of the reasons that we had such a big public relations task, and such negative sentiment, because we'd been seen to, as part of the privatization process, desert the (producing areas). As well as that, that would compound some operational issues that confirmed the theories that we weren't really interested in the (producers), because the payments weren't on time, the paperwork was poor, there was no one in the (producing areas) to get an answer to a question, you know, in many ways we'd confirmed their views. So I guess it was clear to me that we had a group of unhappy stakeholders, we hadn't had the strategic leadership from the board or the top management about a clear future that was acceptable and satisfying to these people, and that really we had a low capability in terms of being able to both manage our existing business well, let alone attain some fairly heady notions about what (Kappa) might be able to do in the future.

236. Strategy Consultant: So let's go back to the start, I mean a fundamental decision related to that. We concluded that it was crucial that we were successful with (producers).

Interviewer: Successful with (producers) in that you were delivering for them or that you were on-side with them, that they were supportive of what you were doing for them?

Strategy Consultant: Both, I mean those two things go together. In the first instance, that you were clear about what it is you are there to do for them. And once you're clear about that, then second priorities within that context. So, that was quite a big shift in the sense that it focused us back on what I used to call the "(producer) mandate."

CEO: You know I'd be probably—I dare say I'd probably be the only top 100 CEO that spends as much time talking to their suppliers, customers, owners. I mean for example, the last three months I've probably talked to two thousand (producers). And what does that mean? It means I spend a lot of my time flying around the (production area), talking to (producers). And we've got all sorts of meetings, we've got consultative mechanisms, we've got custom forums, a whole lot of all that sort of stuff. And I think that's built confidence in direction and people.

237. CEO: Having a lot of great legacy assets that we'd inherited, but basically having a very narrow income base, a bit of a one-trick pony, in the (specific commodity) business, but also a business that was highly susceptible not just to cyclicality, because of (production issues) and basically (production) volume risk, but also political risk, because of the (export monopoly), so the business that we've been in has been a regulated business for a long time, a statutory authority, a privatized company now, (with) a lot

of money, a need to diversify because of cyclicality but also a need to find another life beyond the (export monopoly). And because that (privatization) was a recent event, and even though the domestic market had been deregulated for ten years, there was a big question—well what is it that (Kappa) can do, wants to do?

And so when I came I don't think there was any clarity about the growth strategy for the company, and how we could diversify away from that cyclicality, and also immunize the company from political risk associated with loss of the (export monopoly). So that was the first thing. The second thing was that that uncertainty was magnified and reflected in the stakeholder base, particularly the (producer) base, who were I think very uncertain about this new environment. I mean, for sixty years, (Kappa had been) a statutory authority, (they were) quite comfortable with that, knew what the company did, was happy with basically what the company did, but were asking a lot of questions about, "What does this mean for the (export monopoly)"; we're now in the hands of a public company, a company that's said it wants to become a (stock exchange) listed public company, a company that's seen to be serving two masters,...the shareholder master and the (producer) master, and we're very worried, as the (producers), that our interests are going to be secondary to the interests of the shareholders, and that (Kappa) potentially could be off on a frolic doing all sorts of commercial things and our (export monopoly) will suffer and that's the most important thing to us. So a lot of uncertainty, a lot of questions, a lot of unease about the future direction and the implications of that for their (commodity export monopoly), which is clearly the most important thing to them. And then thirdly the challenge of creating really out of the statutory authority, a now (stock exchange) listed public company with the capability to make money and the capability to do these other two things that we needed to do—articulate a very clear business strategy that was supportable by the market and acceptable and supportable by the shareholder base. So when I first came there was no— certainly no clear view of the board about our future direction, and particularly a direction that sat well, I think, with those other two legs of the stool...what we actually could do, and what the (producers) wanted us to do.

238. CEO: You know as well as capability there's another important ingredient, particularly with a company like (Kappa), that it's got to be consistent with delivering satisfaction and support for the stakeholder groupings, and principally here for the (producers). So not only did we have to have a strategy that was aligned with our capability and feasibly executable, but also have a strategy that was aligned with the interests of our primary stakeholder here, which is really the (producers), who own, control, supply and are key customers of the company. And because we're not just dealing with a purely commercial issue there, we're also dealing with politics

and change and sentiment and the (commodity export monopoly) and a whole range of other things, it was doubly important to make sure that the three legs of the stool—business strategy, stakeholder satisfaction, and organizational capability—were completely aligned.

239. Strategy Consultant: The problem with an organization like this is that it participates across a very large value chain and it touches that value chain at many different points, or potentially touches it at many different points. And if you're talking about the (commodity) industry, you're talking about (production), relationships with (producers), that leads you to think about all the things you might do for (producers). You go on from there to the provision of financial services for and products to them related to the (product), but then you might think about all sorts of other financial services that (you) could provide that might not be related to (production) finance; you go on from there, and that might lead you to think that you should be a bank; you go on from there to risk management, which gets you involved in—and trading, so you might start to think if you weren't constrained that you should be a global commodity trading house, or that you should be a global risk manager type, financial engineer type organization. You then get into marketing of (the commodity) globally, so you might start to think that your job is you should be a global marketer of many commodities and that you can transfer your skills from one commodity across to another. Now, if you're not careful—very, very careful—what you get is a description of a role which will in fact give you a license to do all of those things. And at that point you are in real trouble.

CEO: So it was sorting out all those wild ideas. And then, e-commerce was the go, I mean, God, they wanted us to be an e-portal. You know, we'll be left behind,—settle down, take a (headache remedy).

10 Lambda

Lambda was founded to take advantage of a specific short term investment opportunity, but the investors later prolonged their investment without reviewing their strategy. Subsequently, reactive decisions changed Lambda's underlying purpose and business model.

HISTORY

In the mid-1980s, the Australian government began to reduce the high import taxes that protected much of the local manufacturing sector. One of the larger organizations affected was Predecessor, a focused investor which concentrated on maintaining a dominant market share in the manufacture, distribution, and retail sale of a single family of products. Predecessor operated both as a second tier component producer supplying complex-product manufacturers with these products as original equipment components, and as a manufacturer, distributor and retailer of similar items to the aftermarket. While the original equipment market was much larger than the aftermarket, it was significantly less profitable on a per-item basis, so it was important to pursue both of these opportunities. Because its manufacturing activities were inefficient, Predecessor's strategist regarded the looming loss of protection against imports as the sound of doom, and revised the firm's strategy. The company would now divest its many manufacturing subsidiaries and discontinue sales of original equipment components to complex-product manufacturers, but would retain its national distribution and retailing arms. In the future, it would obtain the products it distributed and sold from the cheapest source—either overseas or local manufacturers. Thus, it would retain the parts of the business that seemed to have the best prospects and dispose of the others.

One of Predecessor's managers believed that a few of the manufacturing businesses still had some potential, at least in the short term. He saw a chance to buy them from Predecessor at the bottom of the market, while investor dismay over impending loss of import tax protection seemed to be at its peak. He believed he could form Lambda, a focused investment vehicle, from five small-to-medium-sized manufacturing businesses then sell it profitably after financial markets had adjusted to the new import tax arrangements. Lambda was a medium-sized firm with one thousand employees.

THE FIRST PHASE: MANAGEMENT BUY-OUT

Lambda's strategic evolution will be divided into two phases. The first phase covers Lambda's formation via a management buy-out in 1986, and its first few years of operation up to the time when the buy-out financier exited. The second phase spans the time from the financier's exit to the case study in 2003.

While he was still a Predecessor manager, the future CEO of Lambda made a financial analysis of Predecessor's manufacturing businesses. Results indicated that with restructuring, five of them could be made into a narrowly-focused entity that would be profitable even when import taxes decreased substantially. The government's policy was to remove the import taxes gradually, so if he organized a management buy-out to acquire these five companies from Predecessor, and restructured them, they could be sold after about three to five years for substantially more than they would cost to buy and reorganize. His strategic concept was to reintroduce Predecessor's old strategy of dominating selected market segments. Lambda would hold a dominant position in the local manufacture of the selected products, so it was likely to remain the restructured Predecessor's sole supplier of them for a few years while imported products slowly declined in price. The combination of Lambda and Predecessor would, therefore, retain Predecessor's pre-existing dominant position in their manufacture, distribution, and sale. Lambda would also inherit Predecessor's ongoing high-volume sales of the same items to complex-product manufacturers as original equipment components.

The Predecessor manager successfully engaged some of his fellow-managers and a financier, and completed a management buyout with himself as CEO. He had a detailed business plan centered on making structural changes to Lambda's five businesses to improve their financial performance. Implementing the plan resulted in the firm's early years being successful and profitable. After a few years, the financier executed the last stage of the original plan by selling out. However, the other investors—the group of former Predecessor managers—preferred to continue their own involvement, so they bought the financier's holdings and became full owners of the company.

THE SECOND PHASE: EXTENDING THE LIFE OF A STRATEGY

Lambda was originally established to pursue a short-term strategy, with perhaps five years of intended life-span. After the investors decided to extend its duration, there was no broad strategic review; Lambda merely continued to operate as it had been doing. However, after a while the CEO did some specific thinking about one issue. Import taxes were decreasing, and so was the size of the Australian market for Lambda's products. Lambda's market share was already about 90 percent. The conventional wisdom among other manufacturers and government experts was that imports were going to create steadily-increasing price competition, and local manufacturers must respond by improving their economies of scale. Those like Lambda that already dominated the domestic market could only increase their production volumes by exporting. The CEO, therefore, decided that Lambda had to export. A simple study indicated that the best opportunity would lie in the US market. Lambda bought a small distributor in the US, but later switched opportunistically to co-distribution with an American manufacturer of complementary products.

Other than the export matter, the CEO did not feel impelled by circumstances to engage in high-level tactical thinking for a number of years. Then a problem arose quite suddenly. From its inception, Lambda had retained the sales pattern in Australia that Predecessor had developed. It sold most of its output to local complex-product manufacturers as original equipment, and the remainder to Predecessor for domestic distribution and retail sale. Viewed as a combination, Lambda and Predecessor occupied the same strategic niche that Predecessor alone had previously enjoyed, but the retail-dominance aspect of that niche was becoming non-viable. Now that some imported products were becoming price-competitive with local production, there was nothing to keep new entrants from directly importing a narrow range of high-margin products and establishing successful retail outlets by undercutting Predecessor's prices. Predecessor responded to this strategic threat by abandoning its relationship with Lambda and inviting both local manufacturers and importers to submit bids for annual supply contracts.

Lambda's CEO still did not revisit the underlying issues, but kept his thinking narrowly focused on the immediate problem. If Lambda competed with importers to remain Predecessor's supplier, margins would be seriously eroded over the years as import taxes declined further. In addition, the firm would have no certainty from year to year of being the successful bidder and having its products distributed. To ensure the continuity of Lambda's business, he persuaded his board to buy an existing small Australian distribution company that competed with Predecessor. A few years later, Lambda bought Predecessor's distribution channel as well, thus acquiring a dominant position in the long-established distribution chain that supplied locally manufactured products to traditional retailers. This reactive decision did not seem to address the possibility that imports of competing goods for sale by non-traditional retailers could gradually make this form of distribution less important. Furthermore, investing in distribution deviated from Lambda's underlying purpose of being focused on manufacturing—a purpose based on the strong preference of all of the shareholders, the board members, and the senior managers. Lambda had lost its focus, and perhaps had also lost its way.

ANALYSIS

Classifying the Strategist

The Lambda CEO was the strategist in this case. Although he worked very closely with his board—made up of former colleagues from Predecessor who joined his management buy-out—he seems to have been the main proposer and analyzer of ideas as well as being the CEO.[240]

Change-Readiness

In the first phase, the CEO approached strategy formation as a formal and detailed forecasting and modeling exercise, undertaken as part of his management buy-out study. He based his strategic analysis on making minimal modifications to a previous model (Predecessor's) that had a successful history.[241] His aim was to achieve a detailed knowledge of the proposed business and produce a correspondingly-detailed plan, in the expectation that this way of approaching strategy formation would minimize risk. In the second phase, he engaged in high-level thinking only when confronted by distinct, immediate problems. The government, the press, and his peers all told him that he had to export, so he exported.[242] Predecessor dumped his company as a preferred supplier, so he sought a solution based on minimum change: he replaced a supply agreement with Predecessor, with a captive distributor.[243]

In summary, he had no specific vision for the company and a fairly short time-horizon. His high-level thinking was reactive and minimal; essentially, he addressed major concerns when it seemed essential to do so. These are characteristics of an adaptive change-readiness.

Cognitive Emphasis

The CEO approached his professional work as a materialist. Success was measured financially, and he tried to ensure it by careful analysis and management. The supremacy of the materialistic imperative was demonstrated by his treatment of the distribution issue. He did not want to be in the distribution industry, because it involved dealing with people of whose behavior he disapproved.[244] However, he believed that he had to engage in distribution to protect and preserve Lambda, so he did what was necessary, and suffered the associated discomfort.[245] So far as egotism is concerned, the CEO showed no noteworthy interest in acquiring or exercising power. He enjoyed performing an executive role successfully, but this was because it was a challenge and he was creating value in a material sense; it was not because of the power he could potentially have wielded.[246] Indeed, he involved his board rather closely and worked with them as a team rather than seeking personal discretion and authority.[247] His explanation of how he came to develop the Lambda management buy-out concept demonstrates that he was not an altruist; he bought the businesses because they were inefficient and poorly managed and could be made successful, not because he felt an over-riding need to preserve employment in those companies.[248] His profile is, therefore, that of a materialist rather than an egotist or altruist.

Cognitive Bias

This analysis has classified the CEO as an adaptive materialist, or Executive. Rather than having a long-term vision, he preferred to wait for issues to become mature and clearly visible, and then he approached them with confidence that he could meet challenges, make decisions, and organize responses however complex. These characteristics fit the Executive type description.

Deconstructing the Strategy

First Phase

In the first phase, Lambda's CEO's basic direction was *plan and execute a management buy-out.* The broad path had one essential thrust: *temporarily reinstate Predecessor's original strategy.*

Second Phase

The event that precipitated the second phase was the investors' decision to extend the life of their investment. Lambda had been simply a short-term investment vehicle until then, and this decision converted it into either a longer-term investment vehicle or an ongoing business, depending on how events unfolded. The decision was not a strategic one, because there was no real strategic thinking; the financier wanted to exit, and the directors made an immediate decision to buy out the financier themselves rather than bring in outside investors immediately. The existing strategy was maintained without review, even though its time-horizon had been reached. This implies that Lambda's second-phase basic direction was *react to events.* The broad path had two essential thrusts, which arose reactively, at different times, in response to different challenges: *export to the United States* and *enter the Australian distribution industry.*

Classifying the Strategy Content

First Phase

To analyze the strategy, we need to identify the channels of influence associated with the individual essential thrusts. The first phase's single essential thrust, *temporarily reinstate Predecessor's original strategy*, involved making it possible to re-establish—for a few years—a small-scale version of Predecessor's traditional strategy. This was to be made possible by a once-only improvement in Lambda's manufacturing competitiveness, to be achieved by gaining control of additional intellectual property, acquiring and closing competing businesses, and improving internal efficiency.[249] It was essentially a process of dominating the supply of scarce resources, and upgrading resource utilization. This, therefore, relied on an internal rational channel of influence.

Second Phase

The second phase's first essential thrust, *export to the United States*, was focused on defending against a growing external competitive threat. The means of response was entering a new market area, to increase economies of scale as a way to achieve a more competitive product cost. This was an external-market-based solution; no substantial change in internal structure, attitudes, processes, or resources was involved, and there was no strategic intention of sequestering a distribution channel in the targeted market.[250] Hence the channel of influence was external rational. The second thrust, *enter the Australian distribution industry*, was aimed at responding to another external threat: the risk of losing the means of distributing the firm's products to the aftermarket. The chosen solution was acquiring a captive distribution channel.[251] Competing in the market for access to resources is an external rational approach; sequestering scarce resources under the firm's own control is an internal rational approach. Hence the first essential thrust was external rational, and the second was internal rational.

Classifying the Strategy Process

First Phase

Strategy process is classified either as deliberate or emergent, depending on whether the strategy was formed in a conscious strategic decision or without such a decision. The first-phase basic direction, *plan and execute a management buy-out,* stemmed from strategic thinking by the CEO-to-be; he was considering forming a new business, and he thought through the strategic issues before making a decision.[252] This means it was deliberate strategy (B1). The essential thrust, *temporarily reinstate Predecessor's original strategy,* came from a conscious strategic decision taken in conjunction with adopting the basic direction, so it was also deliberate strategy (C1). The entire first-phase strategy was deliberate.

Second Phase

The second-phase basic direction was *react to events.* This direction was not adopted consciously, and could only be detected afterwards by retrospective analysis of Lambda's actions.[253] It, therefore, was emergent strategy (B2). The subsequent formation of the two essential thrusts, *export to the United States* and *enter the Australian distribution industry,* must necessarily have been emergent also; it is not possible to form a deliberate essential thrust without there being a basic direction for it to support. Thus, the entire second-phase strategy was emergent, and was an example of purely retroactive strategy formation.

SUMMARY

The Lambda CEO seems to have had a rather strong adaptive preference, and was in a situation where substantial change was inevitable. His behavior was consistent with Chapter 2's prediction that adaptors will tend to be reactive, preferring to be able to see major issues as clearly as possible before making decisions on how to respond. As a result, responses tend to occur as late as possible, and involve as little change as possible. While the CEO was successful in the first phase, he seems to have been less so in the second, and his change-readiness may have been a factor in this.

NOTES

240. CEO: I tend to be the one who brings the—myself and the (chief financial officer) would be the ones who would bring to the board table the bigger picture proposals. But they won't come as a complete surprise to them. They'll come as a result of a discussion that has been evolving, and then finally there'll be an opportunity to say "Hey this is starting to look serious. Let's do this to the next stage of the proposal."

Interviewer: And process can come from anybody, but the spark of the idea, of saying, "This circumstance has arisen. You know, we're doing this in the US and there are these dissatisfactions with it, and although it sounds odd that we'd go out of distribution having gone into it, here's somebody that wants us to do something and it's a good idea because." That would come from somebody in particular who isn't focused on individual issues but is focused on the big picture, and I would have thought it would most likely be you.

CEO: Yes.

241. CEO: I'd been a line manager before going into (mergers and acquisitions), and so I'd operated at a general manager level where you are probably not so much operating at a strategic but more at a tactical level. You are (there), and you have a business, and you're trying to make it better. And I'd operated in that environment, looked at the strategic thinking process going on (higher up) within the organization, and (I'd been) thinking, "Well this is a bit of a dumb way to operate." I could see that from my calculations within the businesses, they each had room for productivity improvement, and I thought and said, "Well, why would you close the business that has room for productivity improvement, if the competitive landscape is such that it's not an absolute disaster?" So my mathematical model would have said productivity improvements can more than offset reductions in (import taxes), and if they're the only two bits of the equation that are changing, then why would you go to the extreme of saying that an asset becomes nothing? And has considerable cost in the process to (close the business).

242. CEO: Well, if you said why export, I looked at the equation of the (falling import taxes in Australia) and said it is clearly recognizing that (the complex product manufacturer) companies need to export, and the driver of (that) behavior is limited market size in Australia. You need scale for manufacturing, you won't get scale out of a market the smallness of Australia, and it was the same for us. Same thing (as) for (Lambda's industry sector's first tier) manufacturers and we said, "Well now, we've done the things that take us from 50 percent of the market to 90 percent of the market. The last 10 percent is always going to be very expensive to get, and very small." And in aftermarket terms, we were the dominant aftermarket player in an aftermarket that was maturing and declining.... So we said it's export or perish, was really the conclusion we came to, because we were in a no-growth market, maybe even in a diminishing market. And we said well, export or perish or go offshore. And we didn't have the capital base to go offshore and we didn't have the confidence of our management skill to pick up our business and translate it into another environment. So we said, "Until you have 50 percent of your output being exported, you would still stay in this base."

243. CEO: And so we would have said we were a manufacturer, and (want) to be a better manufacturer but (also want to) stick to our knitting. But we struck a complication in that process a few years ago, and that complication was that we were heavily dependent for aftermarket distribution on our previous owner, (Predecessor). And we had virtually—they were our sole distributor in (our home market, Australia). They were owned by (a conglomerate, which had purchased the remnants of Predecessor). (This conglomerate) came under huge pressure, decided they would introduce an outsourcing process into the company (through the advice of a global consulting company). They put all of their products that—the key products that (the surviving distribution arm of Predecessor) purchased out to tender. And we looked at that and said, "Hey, there's a real risk we could lose the tender on the core parts of our product, and if that happens we're looking at a very narrow landscape for distribution in this country." So we could be in the same boat we were in (when we were) going into North America here (and found that no-one would distribute our products), only worse, because there are far less players (in the Australian distribution sector). And at that time (an American company) who was a distributor in this country was going through a crisis themselves, and decided that they didn't want to be a distributor. And we saw the opportunity to acquire their Australian distribution business and take that on board as our means of securing our future in distribution in this country.

244. CEO: The move from manufacturing to distribution was an interesting change within the company's culture. I mean clearly you went from a group of people who were focused on design, process design, process control, manufacturing to standards—we live in, as you would know, in (the interviewer's industry) in a very tightly controlled world. And you take a group of people who come from that culture, and expose them to a group of people who, to the extreme can act as (conscienceless opportunists).

    Interviewer: Well, it is an extreme, but it does happen, yes.

    CEO: Barrow boys. And putting those two cultures together has been an interesting challenge.

245. CEO: So yes, we started life as a classic management buy-out of a manufacturer who wants to be a better manufacturer. We looked at where our profit came from in that equation, and we could not give away the aftermarket profitability. When it came under threat, we had to go to Plan B, which was "Protect yourself by morphing," if you like, is the best way to put it, and "Change your identity somewhat in order to protect your core business." So we became a distributor to protect ourselves as manufacturers.

246. CEO: Well the process I went through was to say, "Present state. Possible future state. Is that doable? Is that possible? And could you make money in doing that? And would it be (attractive to a venture capitalist investor)

to do that? And having done that, is there more upside for that business to go forward from there?"… And look, I didn't use anything that wasn't out there in the textbook already, I knew at the end of the day if this was going to be viable, it had to be (attractive to venture capitalists), and I tended to start from "How would I convince (an investment bank) to do this?" And if I could convince a banker to do it, and an investor to do it, then it probably ought to be good for me.

247. CEO: The overall development of strategy, therefore, takes place amongst the board members and because we are intimately involved in running the business and operating it then we, therefore, have the knowledge of that business and we have the knowledge of each other's business activities. So when it comes to acquisitions, changes in strategy, then they would come to our board meeting or be debated at our board meeting or arise from discussions that took place at the board meeting. The carriage of the detail of the strategy tends to be devolved then to myself as chief executive officer—so that's the process that we use.

248. CEO: And what I was observing, (was that) it was that culture of that (Predecessor) organization that was causing people to operate with strategic blinkers. That they weren't prepared to look outside their existing known terms of reference. And so I thought "Well that's not a logical way to go. Could I look again at this as another means of solving the problem using an alternative thinking process?"

249. CEO: I looked at it and said there's a great opportunity there to put the two businesses together…to get productivity savings out of that rationalization of manufacturing…. And if you could do a back-to-back deal and buy out (a small competitor), then we'd acquire the other guy's technology and have a corner on the market…. The game plan for (the second main product) manufacture…it was a very profitable business, probably the most profitable of all the businesses that we acquired at the time. Whilst there were two (relevant) manufacturers, and there still are two (relevant) manufacturers in the country, it was by far the most profitable, and it had not had a lot of attention put into the development of its aftermarket business. And aftermarket had the opportunity to grow even further than it was growing at that time, and it was a very profitable side of the business. So you could take that as the cash cow for the short term, and use its benefits to support the operations that you are rationalizing while you are putting your (first product) manufacturer together. The (third product) plant in (another state) was well developed, had still much more potential for productivity gain, and competed with another (similar base technology) manufacturer here in Melbourne…. And we saw it as an opportunity to acquire and close that operation.

250. Interviewer: I'm not quite clear on why you went into distribution (in the US) except that you couldn't make commercial arrangements that worked with existing distributors.

CEO: That's right, yes.

Interviewer: And that's because they were dominated by the big players?

CEO: Yes. Yes. The existing distributors said to us, we have Brand A or Brand B, why do we want Brand C? And we said well we can't give you an argument other than price and, therefore, we would have been taking our brand into the market in a price fighter position, which we said we didn't want to be in. We said we want to be there on equal terms with A and B in terms of quality. The only way to do that is take a link out of the distribution chain.

Interviewer: OK that sounds a bit different then. Taking the link out was not done though because you strategically wanted to control that link; it was because that link didn't want you.

CEO: That's right, yes.

251. CEO: So, bold move in terms of a manufacturer deciding to go into distribution, but we saw that we had no choice. We were going to be held to ransom by our sole major distributor in the country. We looked at it and we said the risks are unacceptable.

Interviewer: So you said if the market has become contestable, there are two possibilities. One is that you're on the wrong side of where the rewards are

CEO: Yes.

Interviewer: Or alternatively, you might have decided just that the risks are wrong, in that there's not a long term commitment.

CEO: That's correct.

Interviewer: Which of those, or both of those?

CEO: Both of them. We looked at it and said both are there, that this has moved from a long term business relationship where we've got interests in common, to a short term opportunistic process where there will be a winner and there will be a loser, and if you're the person putting the business out to tender, you decide who's the winner and who's the loser

252. CEO: I looked at that and said I totally disagree. (Because) when I calculate the mathematics of the business, that provided you had a workable assumption on productivity improvement, provided you had a workable assumption on technology, and provided you had a view that your workforce could be or was flexible enough to cope with change, then to me there was an opportunity that their exit was my opportunity or our opportunity. And so that was formed out of the knowledge gained of studying and thinking

about the business, and doing "What ifs." I mean my job at the time was merger and acquisitions within (Predecessor), and I looked at it and said, "They're crazy, they're trying to divest of their straw hats in winter and they should have been waiting until summer." And so under those circumstances it was an opportunity there that needed to be thought of.

253. Interviewer: So having then become an exporter (to the US) but a self-distributed exporter, that has some implications for growth prospects through the channel

CEO: Uh huh.

Interviewer: And some things like that. So what else do you do?

CEO: Well the interesting thing with that, the sequel to it is that two years ago we undid that arrangement of being the distributor. We found (that) another manufacturer in North America that we'd been working closely with, who made (an ancillary product), came to us and said, "I've got a bright idea."

Interviewer: Now once you are distributing, are you distributing because it shores up your manufacturing, or are you now in a new business, and you take a fresh look at it?

CEO: Interesting. Yes. Because step one was, we became a distributor to shore up manufacturing. And that made sense. Then we looked at it and said, "Hey, this distribution business is not bad as a business to be in." And that led us to actually become a bigger aftermarket distributor.

Interviewer: So you're distributing other people's products as well as your own.

CEO: That's right, yes. So we moved from taking our own product to market, to becoming a broader distributor, and in fact, last year we took a decision to acquire the only other (nation-wide) aftermarket wholesaler in the country, which was being sold by (the remaining part of Predecessor). And so we bought out the (whole national distribution sector). And that was a case of saying, "Well, over there is one half of the business, which is manufacturing, and over here is now a new arm of the business. We are in distribution and will never get out of it because we have to protect our manufacturing. Do we stay small, or do we get scale on that side of the business?" And so we decided that if there was the risk of low or no growth on this side, then growth could come from that side of the business, still protecting this but we are more profitable with a more robust aftermarket distribution business. So there isn't a vision that you had in (1986, when the management buyout occurred) that stays with you to 2003. I haven't lost the vision of '86, but we have changed with the times.

11 Mu

Mu was a conglomerate investor: it owned a number of stand-alone businesses, but the investments were not linked by any strategic purpose. Its board hired a new CEO to improve the firm's performance, a few years after buying several new subsidiaries in an acquisition spree. Mu's tiny central staff controlled its self-managing subsidiaries by issuing policy directives; that is, by interpreting and updating the underlying purpose of each subsidiary. The key aspect of the case is the distinction between policy and strategy, which became important at two levels: between board and corporate management; and between corporate management and subsidiary management.

HISTORY

Mu's board hired a new CEO because it wanted improved performance from its subsidiaries. The firm owned five unrelated businesses, each of which operated as a stand-alone design, manufacturing and marketing company, producing specialized, durable consumer goods under its own specific brand. The businesses had individual management and administrative structures, so Mu's corporate central office consisted of only ten people including the CEO. Mu had bought some of its subsidiaries in the 1990s without seeming to have a clear intention other than a desire to invest. At the beginning of the case study period, there were no indications that it intended to sell them at some later time (as a "portfolio" investor would do), or that they had been chosen because they formed a coherent group of investments (as a "focused" investor would require), so at that time, Mu could have been described as a "conglomerate" investor. The firm's disappointing overall financial performance led its board not only to employ the new CEO, but also to involve itself in strategy formation by directing that a consultant be engaged. Mu was a medium-sized firm with fourteen hundred employees.

THE FIRST PHASE: GAINING THE INITIATIVE

As usual, the case has been divided into two phases. The first phase covers the time from the CEO's appointment until the board-appointed consultant's recommendations were found to be impractical—a period of somewhat more than a year. The second phase covers the subsequent period when the CEO won support for his own strategy and implemented it.

Soon after he was hired, the CEO found that the board was engaged in activism. The normal practice is for a CEO to propose strategy to the board then, if the proposal is accepted, implementation proceeds subject to the board's ongoing satisfaction. At Mu however, the board called for a strategy consultant to be engaged. The consultant recommended that three of Mu's five subsidiaries be sold immediately, with the proceeds to be used to expand the remaining two, thus converting Mu from a conglomerate into a focused investor. The CEO disagreed strongly with this advice because he deemed it impractical; the three subsidiaries that would be sold were performing poorly, so the disposal process would inevitably be a fire sale, and Mu as a whole would be disrupted financially by the transition. On the other hand, if the subsidiaries were held and improved, Mu would be transformed into a portfolio investor; each subsidiary might be sold eventually, but only for a superior price after it had been raised to peak performance, thus leaving little more to gain by retaining ownership.

The board gave some initial support to the consultant's report and called for an investigation of the feasibility of selling the three divisions. The CEO assigned this project to the business analysis specialist on his central staff. Despite the analyst's initial enthusiasm for the consultant's recommendations, the CEO felt sure that in due course their impracticality would become evident and would be demonstrated to the board. His personal plan was that by the time this occurred he would have established the effectiveness of his own strategy by achieving performance improvements at the subsidiaries. He would then emerge with the board's confidence and with the initiative on future strategy formation in his own hands.

The CEO set to work preparing his strategy for Mu. He developed a vision over a period of three months, and confirmed it through discussions with the management groups of the five subsidiaries. During the same period, he took personal charge of the subsidiary with the worst performance. Over four months, he replaced many members of its management group and set the organization on a path of rapid improvement. This, and other performance improvements he achieved, contributed to his standing with the board. Toward the end of the first phase, the analyst reported that implementation of the consultant's strategy was not feasible because of inevitable and severe transitional difficulties. The board then allowed the whole matter of the consultant's recommendations to die quietly.

THE SECOND PHASE: PEAK PERFORMANCE FROM EACH BUSINESS

As far as the CEO was concerned, it was unthinkable to sell a business without getting a high price because that would be waste, a dirty word to him. His strategic purpose was to improve the performance and market value of each of Mu's five subsidiaries. When eventually he saw diminishing prospects of further rapid improvement, he would be ready to listen to generous offers for them—a typical portfolio investor approach. He intended to achieve this strategic purpose through two measures. First, he wanted each subsidiary to operate as a stand-alone business and have a proven record of excellent performance. This was essential if they were to be salable at high prices. Second, he had to conserve his own time. He believed that a major part of the value he brought to Mu was his ability to fix broken businesses, which he did by gaining insight into how they worked then wielding power to repair what was broken. However, there was a limit to how many businesses he could understand simultaneously, so he was restricted to a small portfolio. The potential size of the portfolio would be increased if his time were managed like the precious resource he believed it to be.

Implementing these measures rested on a common theme: establishing an excellent management team at every subsidiary. He regarded exercising the power of appointment and dismissal as a key part of his responsibility, and it was a distinctive feature of his leadership style. He had a monthly on-site meeting with each subsidiary's management in the context of stringent, standardized financial analysis performed by his staff. At this meeting he sometimes dictated decisions not proposed by the subsidiary's management, such as buying competing firms, discontinuing traditional activities that seemed unrewarding, or taking relatively bold moves in capacity expansion. In one instance, a subsidiary was manufacturing when his analysis showed it was strategically and financially more desirable for it to import the product from a low labor cost country, so he directed it to close its factory. Until then the factory had been its main activity, so in one stroke he transformed it from a manufacturer into a design-and-marketing firm. He saw decisions of this kind as policy matters to be decided at his level, though he was gratified if a subsidiary's managers brought such proposals to him. On the other hand, if he had to tell the subsidiary's managers that they had a product gap or that some competitor was outperforming them in some respect, those managers' days were numbered. Whenever he found weak performance, he acted quickly to replace those responsible.

ANALYSIS

Classifying the Strategist

Change-Readiness

The CEO established a vision for Mu in the first three months after he was appointed.[254] Over his first few years, he made sweeping structural changes in some of the subsidiaries in pursuit of that vision.[255] This approach—giving first priority to forming a vision, then moving toward it regardless of the required scale of change[256]—is characteristic of an innovator. It shows both an emphasis on the long term over the short term, and tolerance for risk and discontinuous change.

Cognitive Emphasis

The CEO had a history of taking frequent, powerful actions: restructuring the management of one subsidiary and closing its factory; instructing another to expand its factory and enter a new market;[257] and often dismissing executives as he instilled the desired emphasis on strong performance and quick action.[258] In his interview, he appeared to take pride in these personal actions. This is the profile of an egotist.

Cognitive Bias

It has been observed in the previous sections that the CEO was an innovative egotist, or Entrepreneur. The type description fits his behavior quite well. However, he accepted that in business, it is appropriate to use a detailed financial scorecard to track progress, and he made a point of doing this.[259] The result was an Entrepreneur with a veneer of materialism.

Deconstructing the Strategy

First Phase

The CEO's first-phase basic direction was *take command and gain the initiative with the board.* The broad path was extremely simple, having just one essential thrust: *privately develop a strategy and begin implementing it.*

Second Phase

In the second phase, the basic direction was *manage Mu as a portfolio investor.* The broad path had two essential thrusts: *optimize each subsidiary as a stand-alone business* and *conserve the CEO's time.*

Classifying the Strategy Content

First Phase

Our next step is to identify the channel of influence associated with each essential thrust of the strategy. The only first-phase essential thrust, *privately develop a strategy and begin implementing it,* tells us how the CEO intended to establish a constructive relationship with the board. He already knew that the board was tending to focus on an unworkable strategic concept.[260] He began implementing the early steps of his own strategy, intending that by the time the board's strategy became discredited, the effectiveness of his own would be starting to become evident[261]—and this plan was successful.[262] The essential thrust was aimed at creating standing for the CEO with the board and using that standing to get his strategy adopted.[263] Because the board is a proxy for the shareholders, the channel of influence was shareholder social.

Second Phase

In the second phase, the first essential thrust was *optimize each subsidiary as a stand-alone business.* This was aimed at making Mu's subsidiaries attractive investment opportunities for external investors.[264] A rational external investor would value an opportunity according to the investment's potential and how long it would take to realize it. A less-rational investor would be especially attracted to an opportunity that was already polished and well-exhibited. The first thrust, aimed at optimizing the performance of each of Mu's businesses, was essentially maximizing the market value of what might be considered Mu's trading stock—its subsidiaries. It was, thus, a marketing activity, designed to attract less-rational investors; that is, it relied on an external social channel of influence. The second essential thrust, *conserve the CEO's time,* was aimed at getting the greatest possible return from a limited resource that was difficult to replicate.[265] This is a classic example of the reasoning used in the Resource-Based View approach to strategy; that is, it is based on an internal rational channel of influence. Thus, the first essential thrust was external social, and the second was internal rational.

Classifying the Strategy Process

First Phase

We classify each element of the strategy as deliberate or emergent, depending on whether it was formed in a conscious strategic decision. The first-phase basic direction was *take command and gain the initiative with the board.* The CEO considered from the start that the consultant's recommendation was not feasible, so his plan was to prepare for the time when this became obvious to the board. This is strategic thinking, so the decision he made to follow that approach must inevitably have been deliberate strategy (B1). By the same reasoning, the essential thrust, *privately develop and begin implementing a strategy*, was also adopted consciously and was deliberate strategy (C1). The entire first-phase strategy, therefore, was deliberate.

Second Phase

The second-phase basic direction was *manage Mu as a portfolio investor.* The CEO indicated that his first conclusion when he began looking at Mu was that the subsidiaries were structurally and operationally below his expectations. Fixing these faults would make Mu more profitable and its subsidiaries more valuable. Meanwhile it was unthinkable to sell any subsidiary because it would imply accepting a price far below the potential worth.[266] This constitutes strategic thinking, and it led to adopting the basic direction, so this was an example of deliberate strategy (B1). The first essential thrust, *optimize each subsidiary as a stand-alone business,* arose as part of the CEO's plans to implement the basic direction. He indicated that he thought of Mu as a group of stand-alone businesses, each of which might be sold if it ran out of performance-improvement potential and the right price were offered.[267] This indicates that the first thrust was deliberate strategy (C1). The second essential thrust was *conserve the CEO's time.* This matter was discussed in detail in his interview, and he confirmed his awareness that his time would always be a scarce strategic resource and, therefore, a limitation on Mu's potential growth, because of the specific way he chose to run the firm. The thrust, therefore, was deliberate strategy (C1). In summary, the entire second-phase strategy was deliberate.

SUMMARY

Mu's CEO had a challenging immediate problem just after he was appointed: the board involved itself in strategy-formation. This reduced the traditional role of the CEO, and it also seemed to him that the board's collective skill in strategy formation was less than his own. Because there was no question that the board had the power to form strategy if it chose to exercise it, the CEO recognized a need to act carefully. He proceeded fairly skillfully and quite successfully to gain power over his traditional domain.

Whilst he carefully guarded the boundary between his board's policy domain and his own strategy domain, when it came to overseeing Mu's subsidiaries the CEO tended to stretch the boundary between the policy and strategy domains to extend the one he personally controlled: the policy domain. He acknowledged in his interview that the strategy of each subsidiary was a matter for its own managers to address, not for him to dictate. Nevertheless, in practice he often made decisions that encroached into the strategy area. This is perhaps an unavoidable tendency. Expecting an Entrepreneur to refrain voluntarily from exercising power in a major available field may be unrealistic.

The Mu case illustrates the role of the CEO in bringing purpose and vision to an organization. When a board appoints a CEO, it chooses a direction, whether or not it recognizes that direction at the time.

NOTES

254. CEO: How did we get to the vision? I guess when I arrived here, it probably took three months to work out what I was going to do with it, for a start.

255. CEO: And the first thing was that until we had the operational stuff sorted out, there was no point in us thinking about growth. And so…(reference to passage of three to four years)…it really took that long to get the operational stuff sorted out. Along the way, there were things that were just so obvious that if you didn't do this, you weren't going to get to there and you weren't—sort of a cliché, but it's getting the ducks lined up.

256. Interviewer: I think from what you've said, you tend to look at the costing, to see where something's wrong.

     CEO: I do.

     Interviewer: And you find—

     CEO: And if it can be improved. That's the crux.

     Interviewer: But the something wrong equals an opportunity.

     CEO: Yes.

     Interviewer: And therefore, something wrong means a need for change, and the need for change is what I'd like to focus on now because some people change it by fixing it, other people change it by starting again. And I think I know which of those you do, but I'd like you to just explain that.

     CEO: It can be a bit of both; it really depends. I mean (the third business area), we fixed it by changing it, because I couldn't start again because the money had already been spent. With (the fourth business area), the fix has been basically to start again. So I do both.

Interviewer: In the case of (the third business area) I think you said you are starting again, but you're going to amortize your investment first.

CEO: Oh yes, OK, but you know, there's about eight years between drinks there, so it's two separate—

Interviewer: But in effect, your vision is not to be making (the third business area) in Australia.

CEO: No.

Interviewer: And that's something you're doing until you can do something else.

CEO: Exactly. Exactly. And as I said, if I'd have been here we would never have done what we did, because it just doesn't make sense.

257. CEO: I said to (the Strategy Manager), go and help these people, and (the Strategy Manager)'s done it, and they've built up a marketing plan, we know the size of the market, we've interviewed customers, and we've selected our range, and we're on our way. And I'm now looking at a potential acquisition which will make us number one in (the product field) in Australia and New Zealand by a long shot. So from something that was a good idea at (the subsidiary), but not proven, not tested, not thought through, you know, I think we'll probably dominate it.

258. Quotes from the CEO:

I'm quite autocratic.

This guy just wasn't going to get there so we parted company.

There were twelve of them in this head office. Gone. They were just a handbrake on progress.

We had some very ordinary management in there; I've put in an outstanding chief executive.

The marketing manager should have been the one driving it, and he wasn't, so he left.

I ran that business for four months. The bloke that was in there, I tipped him out. I tipped out lots of them.

259. CEO: I like the (key Mu product line) business; I like the (second Mu product line) business. Both (have growth potential), both I think for different reasons can actually make us a lot of money. The (third Mu product line) business is going nowhere, it's GDP (Gross Domestic Product) growth at best, it's got technology issues, it's got import replacement issues, there are a whole lot of things that the (third product line)—although year to

date it's made 16 percent EBIT (Earnings Before Interest and Taxes), last month it made 21 percent EBIT, you can't argue with the business—but it's going nowhere. The (fourth product line) business is really going nowhere. Great brand, you know, it would be an ideal MBO (Management Buy-Out). So I wouldn't spend a lot of time putting stuff on the end of that. The (fifth product line) business, this year will do...20 percent EBIT.... Now, it's a great business, but it's going nowhere.

260. Interviewer: The results of the consultancy were never implemented, and I think you said they didn't make sense to you.

CEO: No.

Interviewer: So you went through a process where the consultant came back with something, and you looked at it and you said this doesn't jell for me.

CEO: No.

261. CEO: There were operational issues that were—every time you kicked a rock, the spiders ran everywhere. There were just operational issues everywhere. (Mu) was what it was, which was a mish-mash of businesses that have been acquired through some—I don't think there was strategy, it was growth for growth's sake. And so it was really just a matter of sorting it all out, but I did it all in my head, to be honest.

CEO: Some of our directors, who have never run a business, really think that we should be growing 30 percent per annum, and you can be in whatever your earlier example was—restaurants.

262. CEO: The board wasn't very cohesive at the time anyway, there were three or four different views about where we should be going and what we were doing, and this was actually a fifth view. So, it didn't have a champion on the board. I certainly didn't agree with it. But there was no one else there that really wanted to embrace it, so, absolute waste of money.

263. Strategy Manager: And we each year, as I said earlier, would do a document for the board, where we'd articulate, and over a period it went from (what came) out of the consultants' report—that we were going to be more focused, (and involved in) less activities—to, over time as the businesses started to improve because of the work we'd done, saying, well, these are good businesses to stay in at the moment, we don't really need to (sell) them off. Maybe we can run them for cash, or maybe we've got a bit more upside in them for these reasons, let's continue with it.

264. CEO: I will never know as much about their businesses as they will. No, no, they've got to provide the vision and how they get to it. Whether it's centrally or whether it's done as a committee, doesn't bother me very much. Because that's their personal style.

Interviewer: So they're selling you their vision.

CEO: Yes.

Interviewer: And if it doesn't work for you then you've got to part company.

CEO: Yes.

265. Interviewer: Now did that methodology, which says "First convince me, I need to have an insight into this before I'm going to invest in it," does that set limits on growth?

CEO: Yes.

Interviewer: And is that a strategic issue for you?

CEO: It's not for me, it is in the minds of a couple of our directors, to be honest.

Interviewer: Most people who are as critical about value-adds and so forth (as you are) have some personal psychological need for growth.

CEO: No. I don't.

Interviewer: Would you have that if the company were a lot smaller?

CEO: No.

Interviewer: I can see in any case if you did have such a drive, you would reach a point where you would terminate it anyway because you do want to be able to run the bits of the business yourself.

CEO: Exactly.

Interviewer: So there is a limit to growth, but you're not there yet, particularly if you got rid of some of the things that take time rather than make a contribution.

CEO: Sure.

266. Excerpt from the original case study report: In contrast with the strategy manager, the CEO had always thought it self-evident that the consultants' report was unachievable in practical terms. He approached the situation with a "strategic vision" different from that of the consultants. As a result he found the concept of disposing of poor-performing businesses in an "as is" condition unappealing, simply because he could clearly see how to improve them and was highly confident that he could execute this task. He saw the legacy of fairly poor-performing businesses he had inherited as a personal challenge, and was repelled by the idea of selling them without capturing the financial gains to be made through bringing them into line with his expectations; this would be "waste," a viscerally offensive concept. On the other hand, the consultants' claims that focus on the two preferred business areas would immediately result in sustained, compounded annual

growth rates in the 30 percent range seemed to him unconvincing. Hence, the consultants' report did not capture the CEO's heart and mind. His priority was to fix the businesses he had, which he was quite sure he could bring about in a few years, without much risk of failure or underperformance. He, therefore, was confident he could achieve a number of years of pronounced year-on-year business performance improvements, without requiring the owners to risk an unstable financial performance.

267. CEO: Of those existing businesses, there are two that we like, and the balance we're lukewarm about. The (third Mu product line) business is going nowhere, it's GDP growth at best. The (fourth product line) business is really going nowhere. Great brand, you know, it would be an ideal (management buy-out). The (fifth product line) business...now, it's a great business, but it's going nowhere.

12
Sigma

Sigma was a comparatively small manufacturer in the global chemical industry—an industry dominated by economies of scale. At first sight, this was an almost unviable situation, but a strategic solution was found, based on an ingenious business model.

HISTORY

In 1983, Sigma was a very small chemical manufacturer serving a local market around Melbourne, Australia. The founding entrepreneur wanted to exit, and a young chemical engineer employed by Sigma went looking for an investor to replace him. The engineer rejected a large global chemical company and arranged for a small New Zealand-based chemical manufacturer to buy Sigma. He emerged from that transaction as a shareholder and board member of the New Zealand firm, with personal responsibility for Sigma. Later he took management control of the parent company, and re-named it Sigma. The company was medium-sized; it had twenty-four hundred employees at the time of the case study in 2002.

THE FIRST PHASE: LEARNING THE BUSINESS

As usual, I will describe Sigma's strategic development in two phases. The first phase runs from its take-over by the New Zealand firm in 1983, until the present CEO took management control of the parent firm in 2000. Throughout this phase, he was a board member of the New Zealand parent, and had specific responsibility for Sigma. The second phase begins in 2000 and ends at the time of the case study in 2002.

The first phase was a period of learning for the future CEO. Prior to 1983, he had been an employee of Sigma—a very small, locally-oriented chemical manufacturer that was reliant on import taxes to make it viable. In the mid-1980s, however, it became a subsidiary of a New Zealand firm that was about to emerge from relying on import taxes and begin to compete globally. Over the following fifteen years, the future CEO gave part of his attention to learning to understand the global chemical industry. I will outline what he learned.

Chemical manufacturers needed both raw materials and part-processed multipurpose materials, known as intermediate chemicals, to enable them to formulate final products. Each intermediate chemical could only be manufactured at a world class cost by achieving a certain minimum scale of production. To produce every intermediate chemical it might need in its own plants, at world class cost, a manufacturer would need a full-scale plant for each chemical, even if it only required it in fairly modest quantities. This was clearly impractical. In practice, intermediate chemicals were bought and sold between large chemical companies, so that all of the plants could be of economic size, and in-house use of the intermediate chemicals could be supplemented by inter-company sales. These sales were by economic necessity, priced at the direct cost of production plus a modest margin.[268] As a result, large chemical companies had a two-tiered market for intermediate chemicals. There was the price offered between members of the club—chemical companies that stood ready to sell important intermediate chemicals as well as to buy them—and a different price offered to customers who were outside the club. Those who claimed to be chemical companies but did not manufacture and sell large quantities of intermediate chemicals, were classified as "just a front-of-house," meaning they were not real manufacturers and, therefore, they could only buy intermediate chemicals at outsider prices. This sometimes made them vulnerable to a larger company "going around them" by offering the same final product to the same customers at a lower price.

When he understood these concepts, the future CEO could evaluate Sigma's New Zealand parent's strategy. It was mainly based on identifying attractive markets for chemicals in various countries, then trying to buy small second-hand chemical plants close by at opportunistic prices. The firm manufactured, bought, and sold intermediate chemicals as well as final products, so it was at least potentially a member of the chemical manufacturers' club, but production was spread across multiple product segments selected opportunistically. Practiced by a small manufacturer, this strategy had an important negative effect; the firm had little opportunity to develop new products or strong brands across such a diverse and changeable product range. The future CEO concluded that the strategy was a poor choice for the New Zealand firm. He also believed that execution of the strategy was flawed; serious mistakes were being made. He, therefore, precipitated a reconstruction of the parent firm, from which he emerged as CEO and the largest shareholder. The parent firm was re-named Sigma, its stock-market registration was moved to Australia, the Melbourne plant became the head office, the New Zealand plant was closed, and he formed and implemented his own strategy.

THE SECOND PHASE: A BREAK-THROUGH SOLUTION

The new CEO had already concluded that regardless of its size, a firm could not make a high return on the money it invested in owning and operating chemical plants, but it could from formulating and certifying end products, and from owning significant chemical patents and brand names. Based on this conclusion, he formed a strategy to make Sigma successful. It relied on three points. First, Sigma had to put its main emphasis on the most profitable activities: managing brands, patents, and product formulation and certification. Second, manufacturing had to be continued to a sufficient extent to retain club membership and market credibility. Third, because of its small size Sigma had to limit itself to a single, coherent product thread. He would concentrate the product range on one specific area where Sigma's expertise had been proven.

ANALYSIS

Classifying the Strategist

The second-phase CEO is treated as the only strategist in this case. In the first phase, he had a personal strategy, and in the second, he provided Sigma's strategy.

Change-Readiness

Perhaps the most conspicuous feature of the CEO's change-readiness was the emphasis he placed on his vision. At the beginning of the first phase, he had to find an investor to buy Sigma because the founder had decided to exit. He chose the small New Zealand chemical company rather than a global giant because the effects of joining one of the latter did not conform to his vision.[269] At the end of the first phase, he took command of the New Zealand-based parent company because ultimately it had also failed to satisfy his vision.[270] Treating the vision as primary, and how to implement it as a mere tactical concern, is characteristic of innovators. Other innovative characteristics are evident too: a long-term focus, an acceptance of considerable risks at times (as, for example, when rejecting the global chemical company and aligning with the much-smaller New Zealand one), and a tendency to relish an absence of structure around a problem to be solved.[271] The Sigma CEO appears to have had an innovative preference.

Cognitive Emphasis

The CEO was a man who enjoyed the cut and thrust of business, and over the years made a great deal of money from it. He stated that the money itself was not the motivator—what he really liked was to compete and succeed[272]—but it was evident that his decision criteria were primarily materialistic.[273] He insisted on having the power to pursue his vision, but did not show signs of enjoying power for its own sake, or of seeking to exercise it visibly and arbitrarily, or of having difficulty making genuine delegations of authority.[274] Neither did he attempt to maximize benefits to stakeholders other than Sigma's shareholders. This positions him as a materialist, not an egotist, or an altruist.

Cognitive Bias

Putting the change-readiness and cognitive emphasis together, the CEO emerges as an innovative materialist, or Pioneer. This fits his behavior, since he formed an unusual—indeed possibly unique—vision of how Sigma could succeed and then took the firm there.[275] When journalistic commentators expressed the view that a small Australian-based multinational chemical company could not succeed, he treated their comments as a challenge and an incentive.[276] He assembled a strong, rather stable leadership team,[277] and guided it by treating only the strategic decisions as his personal fief.[278] In the field of tactics, he led open discussions with his top team before making decisions personally. Where operating issues were concerned, he gave only broad direction.[279] This appears to fit the expected behavior of a Pioneer.

Deconstructing the Strategy

First Phase

In the first phase, the future CEO's strategy was personal; he was forming and filling-out a personal vision. The first-phase basic direction, which was largely formed unconsciously, was *learn, grow, and wait.* The broad path was also largely formed unconsciously, and had two essential thrusts: *pay close attention to board deliberations* and *use the Melbourne subsidiary as a cultural and organizational test-bench.*

Second Phase

The second-phase basic direction was *make Sigma a viable global chemical manufacturer.* The broad path had three essential thrusts: *concentrate on product and brand issues, stay in the chemical manufacturers' club,* and *focus on one type of product application.*

Classifying the Strategy Content

First Phase

We must identify the channels of influence that made the strategy effective. The purpose of the first of the first-phase essential thrusts, *pay close attention to board deliberations,* was to build up the future CEO's own understanding. His direction was to learn to be a chemical-industry CEO and his means of learning was partly by watching others.[280] This, therefore, was a project aimed at enhancing his personal internal resource base; in particular, he was learning how the chemical companies and their executives related to each other,[281] implying that this was an internal social project. The second essential thrust, *use the Melbourne subsidiary as a cultural and organizational test-bench,* called for a second form of learning: acquiring leadership experience iteratively by studying and improving a working model of a company.[282] He was again building his personal internal resource base, but this time the resource he was building was his insight into his profession as a leader. This thrust, therefore, was based on an internal social channel. In summary, both essential thrusts were internal social.

Second Phase

In the second phase, the first essential thrust, *concentrate on product and brand issues,* describes part of Sigma's external game-playing strategy against its competitors; it would devote the largest possible proportion of its efforts to the activities with the greatest impact on the outcome of the game.[283] This relies on an external rational channel. The second thrust, *stay in the chemical manufacturers' club,* sets out another part of the posture Sigma was to adopt in game-playing among its peers.[284] Once again, it implies an external rational channel of influence. The third thrust, *focus on one type of product application,* specifies the position Sigma was to adopt in the external market; in Michael Porter's terms it was adopting a "focus" strategy.[285] This once again relies on an external rational channel of influence. In summary, all three essential thrusts were external rational.

Classifying the Strategy Process

First Phase

Each element of a strategy must be formed either deliberately or emergently; there is no third possibility. It has been noted previously that the first-phase basic direction, *learn, grow, and wait,* was largely unconscious. In other words, it did not stem from a single, conscious strategic decision, so it was emergent strategy (B2)—it could only be inferred from subsequent actions.[286] This implies that the entire first-phase strategy was also emergent, because there was no explicit, established basic direction to act as a focus for strategic decisions to adopt specific essential thrusts. In practice, both of the essential thrusts, *pay close attention to board deliberations* and *use the Melbourne subsidiary as a cultural and organizational test-bench,* were also unconscious intentions, so they would have been emergent strategy anyway, even if there had been a deliberate basic direction. In summary, the entire first-phase strategy was emergent, and was an example of purely retroactive strategy formation.

Second Phase

The second-phase basic direction, *make Sigma a viable global chemical manufacturer,* was formed toward the end of the first phase when the CEO had been observing the parent company critically and had become dissatisfied. It was adopted deliberately and explicitly and, therefore, was deliberate strategy (B1).[287] The three essential thrusts, *concentrate on product and brand issues, stay in the chemical manufacturers' club,* and *focus on one type of product application,* were the subsequent and final products of the same period of strategic thinking, so they were deliberate strategy from Process C1. The entire second-phase strategy was deliberate.

SUMMARY

Sigma's CEO began by observing his professional situation objectively, spending as much time as necessary gaining an understanding of its broad context. Then he moved forward as if he were involved in a game, having derived the rules of the game from first principles rather than accepting them as an imposed paradigm. To him, games were about winning without being disqualified; they were not about pageantry, posturing or conforming.

To succeed in his game, the CEO had to interact productively with people who, unlike him, did accept the traditional paradigm for the chemical manufacturing industry. For an innovator in a perhaps mostly adaptive industry,[288] this may have been difficult. He said in his interview that when he explained his business proposals to competitors, "not all of them get it—but enough of them do." Perhaps the global chemical executives who "got it" were less adaptive than their peers and, therefore, less wedded to the prevailing paradigm. However, the CEO also happened to be an unusually pleasant, open, and engaging person. This may have been important to his success, because in most cases, strong innovators are seen by adaptors as rather abrasive.[289]

If the CEO's approach was critical to Sigma's success, his board would eventually need to consider whether it was transferable to a successor. The more unusual and personalized a CEO's style, and the more this style is responsible for the firm's success, the greater the difficulty in maintaining the success after the present CEO moves on.

NOTES

268. Conceptually, the inter-company transfer prices for intermediate chemicals were set at the same level as for intra-company transfer prices. This enabled the companies to make investment decisions without the distortions that would have been created if they had a bias toward in-house production. The result was substantially higher economic efficiency and, therefore, profitability, than would have occurred if an in-house bias had existed.

269. CEO: How we got with the New Zealanders—to some extent (a US-based global company) were trying to buy (Sigma), and ... the originator—the guy who started (Sigma)–and (a global company that was an early investor in Sigma), wanted out. Here's me sitting there with 6 percent of the company, thinking well I've got to do something with this, and I flew up to (the regional office of the global company that wanted to buy Sigma) and talked to (the US-based company), and a guy called (person's name). I can still see him now, Texan, manufacturing guy from (the US-based company). They laugh about it (now), right? But I said "Look, there's a way through this, I've talked to (the Australian federal government's department that oversees foreign investment), I've flown up to Canberra, got involved, you know. If you take a stepwise approach, sure it helps me, I'm an entrepreneur, I can do some things I think are valuable," and the Texan looked at me and said, "No dinky government's ever going to tell (the US-based company) what to do." And I became immediately nationalistic, closed the discussions, came back, found the New Zealanders, and that's history.

270. CEO: So I felt my money was there. I felt they were (messing) it up badly. At first, they were (messing) it up in a small way. Built a sulfur plant in Canada that cost us millions, fifty million bucks, and that hurt. And I reckoned that they'd appointed a guy there that was incompetent, (person's name), and I eventually rose up and said, stop this nonsense, and I want it stopped because it's my dough.

271. CEO: And in fact I can recall (the same US-based company that had wanted to buy Sigma) coming down here. They had a meeting in (their regional HQ) and they sent an emissary from their group, met in our boardroom here, and said, "Look, we've been considering all this, we've decided at our place that you should shut this plant down. We'll be your supplier, and

you'll be very welcome and happy in the club." And we said, "That's very nice of you, thanks very much, we appreciate it, we'll let you know." We never bothered to communicate again on that one.

Interviewer: That would have made you a national distributor then of their products.

CEO: Essentially.

Interviewer: So a sales company.

CEO: And we also—I've seen that they've done that to a guy in (a region of the USA). He was for about three years. Then he wasn't. And I'd seen this situation. So I said to our guys, "I think we'd better go and have this debate in their marketplace, not ours." And we did. And we started delivering (a popular chemical) into the USA.

272. Interviewer: So what are the characteristics that lead to having a vision that's commercially astute?

CEO: Part of it's competitiveness. You want to be competitive. None of it's ever been to stack up the money, none of it's ever been to get wealthy or rich, but it is to succeed, and it is to compete, there's no doubt about that.

273. CEO: Happy to be effectively invested over there (in New Zealand). Sure, I got involved, and I sat on the board, and I looked at it and questioned it and some of that, but we bought stuff off (another chemical company), and bought stuff off another company, and we bought our way into some of this stuff. That's fine, it just was poorly managed, different culture, and had it been a different culture, and been highly successful, I could hardly have been critical.

274. Interviewer: You said self-confidence. Self-confidence to execute the vision once you've got it. Does that mean confidence that the vision's right?

CEO: Yes. Yes, yes, it is true. However, in my view and in fact, I've had to do this several times, be prepared to back up and modify it if it looks wrong.

Interviewer: Yes. How do you find it's wrong?

CEO: Sometimes it's the people won't buy into it. Sometimes they look you in the face and say, "You're kidding." As to all of it or parts of it...parts of it more often than all of it. Sometimes it's just not going to work, it's just not going to deliver. There's a real pragmatism about it; I mean this is business. This isn't art where you've got the vision that you just want to get there and do something like that, it's got to be realistic; it's got to be pragmatic.

CEO: The reason we developed this strategy, is we're better at it. You could make more money if you were really good at pharmaceuticals. But we don't happen to be very good at pharmaceuticals. We've gone out and proven that on a couple of little excursions. The team that we've got tends to think and know about this business—about (Sigma's specialty) business. So we're a business where the leadership team gets up in the morning and think about this stuff. They're well experienced; we know our way around it.

275. CEO: Knowing how it's made and what the chemistry is and being able to interface with the companies that do that and say, hey, has this come off patent, we're either going to make it, or we're going to supply it, and how we're going to work this deal out, how we're going to go. And this is why it's value to you. Now not everyone sees that, but enough of them see it.

CEO: I mean we typically want to handle what I call the last step of manufacture. We're prepared to say to another major company—and we've done it many times this way—the active ingredient is 60 percent of the value of this business. We'll give you that; you get the 60 percent. We have to give that to someone anyway. And there's a cost attached to it. But we want to do this last step. So when it goes into the can, we've had a step in it. ...see, our brand for most of our products is (Sigma). The brand you're relying on is (Sigma). And we'll guarantee the quality of it. If it isn't (right), we'll fix it. And if we (mess) up we'll react to it fast and fix it.

276. CEO: I'm constantly hammered by the analysts in this country...and the fund managers—you can't run a global team. Australian companies can't do that. Now I don't believe that.

277. We might not have succeeded, but we did, and I think issues like persistence, I think longevity—I've got a bit of a different view about how long employees should be in places. I think if they're good and performing, and they can maintain vitality and relevance then it's terrific, stay a long time, right? ... (We disagree with) this idea of churning (staff)—we add to leadership teams, and we have very little turnover. That situation's worked for us. So it's about a people culture, it's about perception of what we can achieve. And I don't know, there's some people might not consider what we've done as successful. We get up every day and fight for it.

278. Interviewer: Where do those ideas come from?

CEO: They'll come from anywhere. They'll come from the guys in the field, not so much the re-salesmen but the management in the field, we need to expand our product portfolio in the following ways. They'll come from the global marketing team. They'll come from me personally, since you know the business, or one of the senior guys personally. They'll say you know, we really are missing the boat here, we need to be doing something.

Interviewer: There's no pattern of who they come from? Probably you more often than any other single person but just anywhere?

CEO: No, there is a pattern. And I've probably been influential in more of them than less of them. But we've got an area in—guy called (person's name) who runs the global marketing business. And (the marketing executive) and his group would tend to come out with them because they're charged with evaluation and ideas of some of that. And you tend to see more that. ... they haven't come up with the overall vision of the total business, but within that vision they're coming through with just product, here's some of the ideas, here's some of the product stuff, right. The overall view, I mean I'm responsible for, and ought to be responsible for. This view that says we're going to have a fairly single focus—we've moved the company from being seventy percent, even in 2000, seventy percent (Sigma's specialty area), to now eighty-five percent (specialty area)—this year, it will go to ninety percent.

279. CEO: And in our business, we've got a lot of matrixing. The guy who runs manufacturing, the guy who runs the business units—that's sales; different guy runs marketing—the guy who runs finance, I mean, they matrix and integrate. And secondly we're a global company so we have to rely on that team. We've got to know and think. If we get a message that something's going off (track somewhere), and that might come because the manufacturing guy's visiting there and sees a thing that just looks off the peg, he's got to be able to feed back, get on the phone, work at it.

280. CEO: Happy to be effectively invested over there (in New Zealand). Sure, I got involved, and I sat on the board, and I looked at it and questioned it and some of that. But we bought stuff off (another chemical company), and bought stuff off another company, and we bought our way into some of this stuff—that's fine, it just was poorly managed, (it was a) different culture—and had it been a different culture and been highly successful, I could hardly have been critical.

281. CEO: We're integrated with all the other companies that are in the business one way or another. Either we supply them stuff, we buy their stuff and/or we compete with them, we do the three pieces.

282. Interviewer: And how did that value arise here? Of saying that you can only work with people you can work with. That's a value now I think of the organization.

CEO: Oh yes, there's no doubt about that.

Interviewer: And it drives your business.

CEO: Culture we call it. But practically the same thing, right.

Interviewer: So how did you get there, how did that come about?

CEO: Oh I guess, partly it's the way I think, and partly the way people who want to work together come together and think, and if you don't feel right—I mean, I'm this bus. (If you don't fit in) then it's better you get off (the bus) and we change it around. So we, you, across time get together, groups of people that feel like this. And then are prepared to work, and work together, and want to aspire to that sort of approach. Now, are we more tempered, skilled today? I think we probably are.

283. CEO: But it is true that market access and the brand is today more important to us than the synthesis, the manufacturing.

284. CEO: The other part—we do last step of manufacturing, last two steps of manufacturing—it's about keeping the quality of it. We have no fear about China being a source of manufactured goods, provided we've got something to do with how that manufacture works. And (we have) got control of where the market access is. We don't need to give someone the opportunity to say, "We'll now come around that. You're just a front-of-house." The brand gives you a lot of security, but it doesn't give you absolute security.

285. (Porter 1980 pp. 35-40).

CEO: But that focus, us being a single focused company, where we get up in the morning and we're really thinking about (Sigma's specialty), is my decision; I don't misunderstand any of that. ...in what we call the New Zealand phase of the company, there were people on the board and the chief executive who felt they wanted a strategy of at least two (types of products), industrial chemical and this (specialty). Sure, I was charging ahead with this piece of it. Now we've got control of the whole thing we're dropping off that (industrial chemical) piece.

286. Interviewer: Just looking at the Australian operation that you were associated with all of that time, how did it become focused and acquire a view that this is the bit that counts and this is the way to do it?

CEO: I think we took—each bit reinforces the next bit. Each step reinforces the next step.

287. CEO: Yes, I guess that successful companies in our industry, if you're the supply side of the industry, function globally. I don't know—well I guess I do know why, if I think about it. The part of the industry that delivers the product to the user, the (chemical product consumer), almost—not almost, is, everywhere in the world, a national piece. The part of the industry that supplies the products to those (local "national" people who in turn supply them to the final users) is international. That's just the way the industry is, you couldn't readily function as a—part of it is the size of the market.

CEO: But that focus, us being a single focused company, where we get up in the morning and we're really thinking about (Sigma's specialty), is my decision, I don't misunderstand any of that. ...there were, in what we call the New Zealand phase of the company, there were people on the board and the chief executive who felt they wanted a strategy of ... industrial chemical and this. ... Now we've got control of the whole thing we're dropping off that (industrial chemical) piece.

Interviewer: You said you started with manufacturing and then decided to add the brand ownership, but why did you keep manufacturing, rather than go to the brand ownership?

CEO: There are degrees of manufacturing, too. That's the other part of the (solution). We don't have to do everything ourselves. We are prepared, and do, link with other parties and do other things, and cross over, and exchange, and all that sort of thing. I think because it's economic to do it, because we can add value at it. If we can't then we tend not to.

CEO: It just was poorly managed ... I felt they were (messing) it up badly... and I eventually rose up and said, stop this nonsense.

288. If an industry is very stable—and oligopolies may be especially prone to being stable—there is a likelihood that adaptors will thrive there better than innovators, who tend to require change.

289. See Appendix 1.

13
An Overview

I explained in Chapter 3 that to compare the strategies of different organizations, we must apply a clear, specific, coherent strategy concept. As long as this requirement is met, the actual concept we choose need not prevent our comparisons from being valid, but it does affect their usefulness. To maximize usefulness, we want our analyses to be generally compatible with the strategy literature, and ideally also with analyses made by other people at other times. The purpose of this book is to offer a strategy concept that makes this possible. The concept focuses on just four crucial aspects of strategy: the decision-maker's way of thinking, the actual content of the strategy, the means by which each aspect of the strategy took effect and the process by which each aspect of the strategy was formed. To make analyses and comparisons of strategies not just feasible but also as convenient as possible, the lower bound of the strategy domain has been set at a high level.[290]

Only the single, highest-level, overall direction the organization takes, and the most focused, direct, and coherent view of what is to be done in pursuit of that direction, are considered strategic. Everything else that is to be done—whatever its scale, scope, and importance—is at most tactical, but the great majority of it is operational. Significant initiatives that contribute materially to implementing the strategy are automatically considered tactical. In practice, there also are other tactical initiatives that are not directly related to strategy. These should be viewed like non-strategic military battles; their existence implies that a significant part of the organization's resources is being consumed by other matters rather than focused entirely on implementing the strategy. There can be valid reasons for doing this. A useful example is enhancing performance through internal changes in processes, organization, or equipment. Such initiatives are the usual means for achieving major improvements in efficiency and effectiveness, but in most cases, they are not strategic because the same organizations have even larger opportunities in the external world and focus their strategies on these. Clearly, major internal improvements may be well justified even if they are not strategic. The main question is whether individual organizations have the capacity to undertake them simultaneously with strategic pursuits.

Analyzing strategy requires insight into the thoughts and nature of the strategist as well as awareness of the observable facts of the case. Making a reliable analysis involves substantiation, examination, and reconciliation of these thoughts, as well as testing the entire analysis for compatibility with each of the properties of the strategy construct set out in Chapters 2 and 3. Consistently adopting the specific analytical steps used in the ten cases analyzed earlier in this book, can provide some structure to this process.

SPECIFIC OBSERVATIONS

This book is about understanding and analyzing strategy. It is not a presentation of research data, which would hardly be a realistic endeavor in any case, on the basis of just ten cases. However, I will make a few comments that might be useful to strategy practitioners. They may also intrigue researchers, who may choose to investigate further.

Strategists

In every case-analysis in this book, the organization's strategist was also its CEO.[291] This is unsurprising because the strategist, by definition, is the person who makes the strategic decisions—the most important and far-reaching decisions that are made within that organization. It would be remarkable if the CEO, the person responsible for the organization's viability and success, did not make all such decisions personally.[292] Naturally, strategists are free to obtain any advice they want, prior to making their decisions. It is the fact of making (or having the power to make) strategic decisions that identifies a strategist, not the analytical or creative thinking that shapes the alternatives. In Chapter 2, we developed a simple typology of strategists' ways of thinking, or cognitive biases, finding twelve possible types. We hypothesized that only six of the types are likely to produce sustained organizational success. Appendix 2 summarizes the results of the ten case analyses, showing that they are consistent with that hypothesis. Every one of the twelve strategists interviewed seemed to conform to one of the six expected types.[293]

I suggested in Chapter 2 that the strategist's type can be expected to affect the strategic decisions that are made. The results in Appendix 2 are consistent with that expectation. Cognitive bias had a major influence on 70 percent of the twenty strategies analyzed. This is a higher percentage than any of the other three influential factors in the strategy-formation model.[294] Clearly, who the strategist is tends to have a profound effect on what an organization's strategy will be.[295] Chapter 2's type descriptions seem to suggest the kinds of organizations and situations that might best suit various types of cognitive bias.[296]

With regard to the first component of cognitive bias, change-readiness, we might hypothesize that adaptive strategists could be more successful than innovators when the organization and its environment were stable, but innovators might do better than adaptors in situations where major change was required.[297] Change was necessary, or at least strategically desirable, at nine of the ten organizations we examined.[298] We classified eleven strategists at those nine organizations:[299] six were adaptors and five were innovators. Were the new strategies chosen by the five innovators more successful than those of the six adaptors? We cannot tell, because the nine organizations' individual potentials were not directly comparable. However, the innovators adopted more aggressive, perhaps riskier strategies than the adaptors.[300] Three of the innovators, but only one of the adaptors, discovered unfulfilled potential in their organizations' situations, resulting in substantial profit improvement.[301] Two of the adaptors were strategically inactive for long periods despite changes in their external environments, and their organizations seem to have been disadvantaged by this.[302] Theta's innovative first-phase strategist held that job for forty years, and he may ultimately have become less attentive to some important operating details than a typical adaptor might have been, which may have disadvantaged his organization.[303] These outcomes seem to show a degree of consistency with the change-readiness hypothesis.

Turning to the second component of cognitive bias—cognitive emphasis—we might hypothesize that materialists (Executives and Pioneers) would suit profit-seeking organizations; altruists (Administrators and Visionaries) would suit religious and charitable organizations as well as the administrative level of government; and egotists (Operators and Entrepreneurs) might be fairly suitable strategists in many situations,[304] but perhaps especially the military, and the political level of government.[305] The results from the case analyses do not seem inconsistent with that hypothesis. Appendix 2 shows that the ten strategists at profit-seeking organizations consisted of four materialists and six egotists. Four of those ten strategists were at small businesses, and all four were egotists.[306] The remaining six were at medium-sized businesses, and four of those were materialists while the other two were egotists. The only strategist who was at a government-owned organization was an altruist.[307]

A particular comment can be made on one specific type of strategist: the Operators (adaptive egotists). The type description and Appendix 1 lead to a hypothesis about this type. Operators may not appeal to most investors or boards for appointment as CEOs, because they are likely to manage organizations by making an endless series of isolated operating-decisions rather than engaging in either tactics or strategy. Many professional investors and directors might regard this as a less-than-optimally-effective approach. The very small sample of cases analyzed seems consistent with this hypothesis: there were only two Operators, and both of them inherited their strategist roles in a small family business (Beta). There were no Operator strategists appointed by boards or professional investors.

Essential Thrusts

After deconstruction, a strategy consists of a basic direction, and a broad path in that direction. A broad path consists of one or more essential thrusts. The strategy concept adopted in this book only recognizes thrusts as components of strategy if they directly support the basic direction. This was expected to result in each strategy having a rather small number of essential thrusts.[308] In practice, all of the twenty strategies analyzed had between one and three essential thrusts, with an average of 2.2 thrusts per strategy. This outcome is in line with the expectation.

Channels of Influence

In Chapter 2, we derived a total of six generic channels of influence, or ways that strategy can take effect. Proposition 6 in Chapter 3 specifies that each of a strategy's essential thrusts relies on one primary channel of influence to bring about the intended outcome. We expect this channel to match the particular circumstances that applied: that is, the organization's environment. We can hypothesize that sometimes a particular type of organization will seem to emphasize a specific channel of influence, due to the environment that usually applies to such organizations. The results show some consistency with this hypothesis. Five of the ten organizations analyzed were second, third or fourth tier suppliers to complex product manufacturers: that is, they were component manufacturers. Consequently, they sold most or even all of their production to higher-tier manufacturers through negotiations with their customers' professional purchase-agents and engineers.[309] Traditional economic theory suggests that in an established, competitive, unregulated market consisting only of skilled, informed professional sellers and buyers, the "rational man" economic model would be likely to apply, so channels of influence would predominantly be rational.[310] This was borne out in practice. Ninety-one percent of the five component manufacturers' essential thrusts were rational,[311] while for the other five organizations only 48 percent of essential thrusts were rational.[312] Of course, these latter five organizations were of various types and their individual environmental circumstances varied widely.

Three of the ten organizations had adopted essential thrusts aimed at influencing their shareholders. There were five such thrusts in total, and all of them used a shareholder social channel of influence. There were no thrusts directed toward influencing shareholders by rational means. Shareholder rational was the only one of the six generic channels of influence introduced in Chapter 3 that was not used in practice in any of the cases analyzed.

Strategy Processes

Chapter 3 explains that any component of any strategy must either be adopted deliberately (through a conscious strategic decision) or emergently (as an implicit, unintended outcome of one or more non-strategic decisions). Where a basic direction is adopted deliberately, there may still be emergent essential thrusts supporting it. Alternatively, an entire strategy may develop emergently; these have been termed "purely retroactive" strategies.[313] Four of the twenty strategies analyzed in this book were purely retroactive, meaning that their basic directions and all of their essential thrusts were formed without strategic decisions.[314] The other sixteen strategies had deliberate basic directions, and all of their essential thrusts were deliberate as well. However, two of Beta's second-phase essential thrusts only became deliberate when they were adopted consciously by the strategist after they had formed and taken effect emergently.[315]

An unexpected feature of all twenty strategies was the degree of control that the strategists seem to have had over strategy formation. According to the explanations given in interviews, every component of every strategy was formed with the active involvement of the strategist. This contrasts with Chapter 3, where it is suggested that strategy will sometimes be formed inadvertently due to decisions by various people in different parts of an organization, and only be discovered by the strategist later, if at all. Two points should be noted about this observation, however. First, the characteristics of the organizations may have favored this outcome. None of them was large (all were small or medium-sized), none could be described as bureaucratic, and all were under the rather active supervision of their strategists. Second, my only informants were the strategists themselves and a few senior staff-members selected for interview by those strategists personally, so a possibility of informant-bias exists.[316] Despite these points, the results suggest that active control of strategy formation by CEOs is a very common practice, even where the final strategy is emergent.[317]

Final Comments

This book is intended to offer strategy practitioners, and others interested in the subject, a cohesive and coherent understanding of the strategy concept. This understanding can be used to penetrate and compare the strategies of widely-differing organizations, or even personal strategies. Reliable analysis, however, requires not only understanding the strategy concept, but also having a sufficient supply of reliable data. The tools developed in this book can help in testing the adequacy and internal consistency of the available data, but they cannot compensate for an absence of data.

It will be evident by now that while acquiring an understanding of strategy theory is not excessively difficult, understanding specific real-world strategies may often be more challenging, primarily due to data-access issues. The case analyses in this book were based on long, frank, fully-transcribed interviews with CEOs, and often with other top-team members as well. Investors, suppliers, and competitors sometimes have to rely on less direct—and therefore less efficient—data acquisition techniques. However, the information can usually be obtained.

NOTES

290. Obviously, the size of the strategy analysis task increases rapidly if we increase the depth of the strategy concept by lowering the cut-off line between strategy and tactics.

291. In the second phase of the Beta case, the CEO and his brother (who was co-director of the company) jointly formed a gestalt strategist. In every other instance, the strategist was the CEO acting alone.

292. Decisions can of course be made passively, invisibly, or retrospectively—see Wrapp (1967) for some interesting discussion of this.

293. Only five of the six types were represented—no Visionary (innovative altruist) was found in the ten cases. There was no indication that any of the strategists belonged to one of the three cognitive emphases excluded from the typology: theorists, mystics, and aesthetes. However, as explained in Chapter 2, that is not to say that these three types do not sometimes lead—or more likely, found—organizations. This is especially true of theorists. The typology excludes them because we hypothesized that they may not be as successful as the other types, not because they may not sometimes attempt the role.

294. The model is illustrated in Figure 1. Appendix 2 shows that external environment was a primary influence in 60 percent of the strategies analyzed, underlying purpose in 25 percent, and internal environment in 25 percent.

295. In the real world most strategists are not able to appoint themselves to suitable jobs; they must convince an organization's policy-maker—usually a board of directors—to appoint them. The outcome of the appointment process depends on many factors, and does not necessarily result in a perfect matching of personality types to specific challenges.

296. As explained in Chapter 2, for the purposes of this book, a cognitive bias consists of a change-readiness and a cognitive emphasis.

297. Michael Kirton, the originator of the adaptor/innovator concept, said that the adaptor "is essential to the functioning of the institution all the time, but occasionally needs to be 'dug out' of his systems." He said that the innovator "in the institution is ideal in unscheduled crises, or better still to help to avoid them, if he can be controlled" (1976).

298. The exception was Delta. Delta's key strategic issue—whether to function as public infrastructure or as a profit-oriented enterprise—was a matter of personal or political judgment: there does not seem to have been a technically-correct answer. In their first phases, Alpha and Theta were in start-up situations and, therefore, required an initial strategy. Beta, Gamma, Epsilon, Theta in its second phase, Kappa, Lambda, and Sigma in its first phase all required new strategies, because the effects of economic reforms adopted by the Australian federal government invalidated their old ones. Mu in its first phase had a form of initial power-struggle between board and CEO. In their second phases Alpha, Mu, and Sigma did not so much require new strategies, as they had unfulfilled potential to improve their performances substantially; and all of them had strategists who recognized and pursued these potentials.

299. Two other strategists at those nine organizations (Gamma first phase and Epsilon first phase) were not interviewed or classified.

300. This proves nothing of course, since it was one of the indicators we used in classifying them as innovators.

301. The innovators were at Alpha, Mu, and Sigma in their second phases. The adaptor was at Lambda in its first phase.

302. These were Beta in its first phase, and Lambda in its second phase.

303. His successor's initial discussions with customers indicated that they had been reducing their purchases from Theta, because they considered the standard of service unsatisfactory. Appendix 1 tells us that innovators are "capable of detailed routine (system maintenance) work for only short bursts (and are) quick to delegate routine tasks." (Kirton 1976). The first-phase Theta strategist said that he had stayed in his role at Theta for so long, despite its poor fit to his personality, because of "sheer greed."

304. Obviously, cognitive bias is likely to influence personal style. I do not mean to suggest that egotists will necessarily succeed in situations where their will to power causes dissonance with other people involved. This may be the Achilles' heel of egotists.

305. Eduard Spranger, the originator of our cognitive emphasis typology, named egotists the "political" type because the political level of govern-

ment seemed to provide the purest and most effective outlet for their will to power (Spranger 1928 pp. 188-189).

306. We can only speculate on why all of the small-business proprietors were egotists; perhaps some egotists are more suited to having full control of a small organization than they are to having a lesser role in a larger one.

307. The only interviewed strategist who was at a non-profit association was a materialist, which seems reasonably consistent with the nature of the association concerned—it was a national coordinating and lobbying group for manufacturing businesses.

308. The smallness of this number is a result of Propositions 2 and 5 in Chapter 3, which require that the strategy as a whole, and each of its essential thrusts, are single coherent concepts and each thrust directly addresses the delivery of the basic direction. As explained in Chapter 3, the strategy concept was intentionally defined in a way that kept the number of thrusts small, to make strategy analysis feasible and reasonably convenient.

309. These were Alpha, Beta, Gamma, Theta, and Lambda.

310. Because buyer and seller are both expected to be skilled, knowledgeable, and under continuous observation by their owners or boards, there seems relatively little opportunity for less-rational (social) factors to influence behavior, leaving games theory as the best available technique for each player to use.

311. Of twenty-three thrusts, fifteen were external rational and six were internal rational.

312. Of twenty-one thrusts, eight were external rational and two were internal rational.

313. (Mintzberg 1977). Mintzberg noted that it is not unusual for organizations to recognize their purely retroactive strategies after they have formed, and adopt them formally—which transforms them from emergent into deliberate strategy.

314. They were Alpha second phase, Beta first phase, Lambda second phase, and Sigma first phase. None of these purely retroactive strategies appeared to have been transformed into deliberate strategy by subsequent strategic decisions.

315. There has been vigorous dissension in the strategy literature about how common emergent strategy is versus deliberate strategy. See Pascale (1984), Mintzberg (1990, 1996) and Ansoff (1991).

316. Conceivably the strategists nominated like-minded executives for the supplementary interviews. Even truthful interviewees can only describe what they perceive as the truth; they may misunderstand or be misinformed.

317. That is, the strategist is often in firm control of all of the important decisions being made in the organization. See the second phase of the Alpha case for an example of how this situation can coexist with emergent strategy formation.

APPENDIX 1: ADAPTORS AND INNOVATORS

ADAPTORS	INNOVATORS
Qualitative Characteristics	
Characterized by precision, reliability, efficiency, methodicalness, prudence, discipline, conformity. Seeks solutions to problems in tried and understood ways. Reduces problems by improvement and greater efficiency, with maximum of continuity and stability. Liable to make goals of means. Challenges rules rarely, cautiously, when assured of strong support. Tends to high self-doubt. Reacts to criticism by closer outward conformity. Vulnerable to social pressure and authority; compliant. Seems impervious to boredom, seems able to maintain high accuracy in long spells of detailed work.	Seen as undisciplined, thinking tangentially, approaching tasks from unsuspected angles. Queries problems' concomitant assumptions; manipulates problems. Is catalyst to settled groups, irreverent of their consensual views; seen as abrasive, creating dissonance. In pursuit of goals treats accepted means with little regard. Often challenges rules, has little respect for past custom. Appears to have low self-doubt when generating ideas, not needing consensus to maintain certitude in face of opposition. Capable of detailed routine (system maintenance) work for only short bursts. Quick to delegate routine tasks. (Kirton 1976)
Accept consensus and constraints with emphasis on limiting disruption. Focus on immediate efficiency. Incorporate new material into existing structures or policies to improve efficiency.	Reject the usual perception and redefine the problem – perhaps in a way that others do not comprehend. Focus on long-term gains. Have less need for structure. Seize opportunities to set new policies. Are ready to risk destruction of the existing paradigm. (Kirton 2003 p. 55)
Strong Correlations	
Less impulsiveness (Tellegan's Research Scale) Less flexibility, less social presence/self confidence (California Psych. Inventory) More need for structure (Wesley Total)	More impulsiveness More flexibility, more social presence/self confidence Less need for structure (Gryskiewicz 1982)
Less tolerance of ambiguity (Budner 16 item) More need for clarity (6 item Ivancevich and Donnelly) Less self-esteem (10 item Rosenberg)	More tolerance of ambiguity Less need for clarity More self-esteem (Keller & Holland 1978)
Less risk-taking (Jackson Personality Inventory) Less sensation-seeking (ASTI)	More risk-taking More sensation-seeking (Goldsmith 1984)

APPENDIX 2: SUMMARY OF CASE ANALYSES

Organization	Phase	Strategist	Influences	Basic Direction	Essential Thrust 1	Essential Thrust 2	Essential Thrust 3
Alpha (40) Component manufacturer	1	Entrepreneur	Cog. Bias	Deliberate	Ext Soc, Deliberate	Ext Rat, Deliberate	Int Rat, Deliberate
	2	Entrepreneur	Cog. Bias	Emergent	Ext Rat, Emergent	Ext Rat, Emergent	
Beta (40) Component manufacturer	1	Operator	External, Cog. Bias	Emergent	Ext Rat, Emergent		
	2	Operator	External, Cog. Bias	Deliberate	Ext Rat, Deliberate	Ext Rat, Deliberate	Ext Rat, Deliberate
Gamma (50) Component manufacturer	1	Not interviewed	External	Deliberate	Ext Rat, Deliberate	Ext Rat, Deliberate	Ext Rat, Deliberate
	2	Entrepreneur	External, Cog. Bias	Deliberate	Ext Rat, Deliberate	Ext Rat, Deliberate	Ext Soc, Deliberate
Delta (90) Infra-structure	1	Administrator	Cog. Bias	Deliberate	Int. Soc, Deliberate		
	2	Administrator	Cog. Bias	Deliberate	Ext Rat, Deliberate	Ext Rat, Deliberate	Ext Rat, Deliberate
Epsilon (200) Industry Association	1	Not interviewed	External, Und. Purp.	Deliberate	Ext Rat, Deliberate	Share. Soc, Deliberate	Share. Soc, Deliberate
	2	Executive	External, Cog. Bias	Deliberate	Int. Rat, Deliberate	Ext Rat, Deliberate	Ext Soc, Deliberate
Theta (500) Component manufacturer	1	Entrepreneur	External	Deliberate	Ext Rat, Deliberate	Ext Rat, Deliberate	
	2	Executive	Und. Purp.	Deliberate	Int. Rat, Deliberate	Int Rat, Deliberate	Int Rat, Deliberate
Kappa (600) Asset manager	1	Executive	Und. Purp, Internal	Deliberate	Share. Soc, Deliberate	Int Soc, Deliberate	
	2	Executive	External, Und. Purp, Internal	Deliberate	Share. Soc, Deliberate		
Lambda (1000) Component manufacturer	1	Executive	External, Cog. Bias	Deliberate	Int. Rat, Deliberate		
	2	Executive	External, Cog. Bias	Emergent	Ext Rat, Emergent	Int Rat, Emergent	
Mu (1200) Portfolio investor	1	Entrepreneur	Und. Purp, Cog. Bias	Deliberate	Share. Soc, Deliberate		
	2	Entrepreneur	Internal, Cog. Bias	Deliberate	Ext Soc, Deliberate	Int Rat, Deliberate	
Sigma (2400) Chemical manufacturer	1	Pioneer	External, Cog. Bias, Internal	Emergent	Int. Soc, Emergent	Int Soc, Emergent	
	2	Pioneer	External, Cog. Bias	Deliberate	Ext Rat, Deliberate	Ext Rat, Deliberate	Ext Rat, Deliberate
Abbreviations	Cog. Bias = cognitive bias; Und. Purp. = underlying purpose; Ext Rat =external rational; Int Rat = internal rational; Share. Rat = shareholder rational; Ext Soc = external social; Int Soc = internal social; Share. Soc = shareholder social.						

Bibliography

Allison, Graham Tillett, Jr., 1971, *Essence of decision: Explaining the Cuban missile crisis*, Little Brown, Boston.

Allport, Gordon Willard and Vernon, Philip Ewart, 1930, *Study of values*, Houghton Mifflin, Boston.

Allport, Gordon Willard, Vernon, Philip Ewart and Lindzey, Gardner, 1960, *Study of values*, Houghton Mifflin, Boston.

Andrews, Kenneth Richmond, 1971, *The concept of corporate strategy*, Dow Jones-Irwin, Homewood.

Andrews, Kenneth Richmond, 1980, 'Directors' responsibility for corporate strategy,' *Harvard Business Review*, vol. 58, no. 6, pp. 30-42.

Ansoff, H. Igor, 1965, *Corporate strategy*, McGraw-Hill, New York.

Ansoff, H. Igor, 1991, 'Critique of Henry Mintzberg's 'The Design School: Reconsidering the basic premises of strategic management',' Strategic Management Journal, vol. 12, no. 6, pp. 449-461.

Barnard, Chester Irving, 1940, 'Comments on the job of the executive,' *Harvard Business Review*, vol. 18, no. 3, pp. 295-308.

Barnett, Michael L., 2007, 'Stakeholder influence capacity and the variability of financial returns to corporate social responsibility,' *Academy of Management Review*, vol. 32, no. 3, pp. 794-816.

Bower, Joseph Lyon and Doz, Yves, 1979, 'Strategy formulation: A social and political process', *Strategic management: A new view of business policy and planning*, D. E. Schendel and C. W. Hofer, Little, Brown, Boston, pp. 152-166.

Bower, Joseph Lyon and Gilbert, Clark G., 2007, 'How managers' everyday decisions create or destroy your company's strategy,' *Harvard Business Review*, vol. 85, no. 2, pp. 72-79.

Burrell, Gibson and Morgan, Gareth, 1979, *Sociological paradigms and organisational analysis: Elements of the sociology of corporate life*, Heinemann, London.

Busenitz, Lowell W. and Barney, Jay B., 1997, 'Differences between entrepreneurs and managers in large organizations: Biases and heuristics in strategic decision-making,' *Journal of Business Venturing*, vol. 12, no. 1, pp. 9-30.

Buttner, E. Holly & Gryskiewicz, Nur, 1993, 'Entrepreneurs' problem-solving styles: An empirical study using the Kirton adaption/ innovation theory,' Journal of Small Business Management, vol. 31, no. 1, pp. 22-31.

Chamberlain, Geoffrey Paul, 2003, *What has to come together before a strategy can? Identifying the conditions precedent for strategy formation in Australian companies*, Unpublished DBA thesis, RMIT, Melbourne, pp. 449.

Chamberlain, Geoffrey Paul, 2006, 'Researching strategy formation process: An abductive methodology,' *Quality and Quantity*, vol. 40, no. 2, pp. 289-301.

Chan, David, 1996, 'Cognitive misfit of problem-solving style at work: A facet of person-organization fit,' Organizational Behavior and Human Decision Processes, vol. 68, no. 3, pp. 194-207.

Chandler, Alfred Dupont, Jr., 1962, *Strategy and structure: Chapters in the history of the industrial enterprise*, MIT Press, Cambridge.

Christensen, C. Roland, Andrews, Kenneth Richmond and Bower, Joseph Lyon, 1973, *Business policy: Text and cases*, Richard D. Irwin, Homewood.

Christensen, C. Roland, Andrews, Kenneth Richmond, Bower, Joseph Lyon, Hamermesh, Richard G. and Porter, Michael E., 1987, *Business policy: Text and cases*, Richard Irwin, Homewood.

Clapp, R. G., 1993, 'Stability of cognitive style in adults and some implications, a longitudinal study of the Kirton Adaption-Innovation Inventory,' Psychological Reports, vol. 73, pp. 1235-45.

Clausewitz, Carl, von, 1968, *On war*, Penguin, London.

Collins, Orvis F., Moore, David G. and Unwalla, Darab B., 1964, *The Enterprising Man*, Bureau of Business and Economic Research, Graduate School of Business Administration, Michigan State University, East Lansing.

Cyert, Richard Michael and March, James Gardner, 1963, *A behavioral theory of the firm*, Prentice Hall, Englewood Cliffs.

Donaldson, Thomas and Preston, Lee E., 1995, 'The stakeholder theory of the corporation: Concepts, evidence, and implications,' *Academy of Management Review*, vol. 20, no. 1, pp. 65-91.

Fahey, Liam, 1986, 'Evaluating the research on strategy content,' *Journal of Management*, vol. 12, no. 2, pp. 167-183.

Foxall, Gordon R. & Payne, Adrian F., 1989, 'Adaptors and innovators in organizations: A cross-cultural study of the cognitive styles of managerial functions and subfunctions,' Human Relations, vol. 42, no. 7, pp. 639-650.

Goldsmith, Ronald E., 1984, 'Personality characteristics associated with adaption-innovation,' *Journal of Psychology*, vol. 117, no. 2, pp. 159-65.

Gryskiewicz, Stanley S., 1982, 'Creative leadership development and the Kirton Adaption-Innovation Inventory', Occupational Psychology Conference of the British Psychological Society, Brighton, UK

Hambrick, Donald C. and Mason, Phyllis A., 1982, 'The organization as a reflection of its top managers,' *Academy of Management Proceedings*, pp. 12-16.

Hillman, Amy J. and Hitt, Michael A., 1999, 'Corporate political strategy formulation: A model of approach, participation and strategy decisions,' *Academy of Management Review*, vol. 24, no. 4, pp. 825-842.

Hofer, Charles W. and Schendel, Dan E., 1978, *Strategy formulation: Analytical concepts*, West Publishing, Saint Paul.

Huff, Anne Sigismund and Reger, Rhonda Kay, 1987, 'A review of strategic process research,' *Journal of Management*, vol. 13, no. 2, pp. 211-237.

Keller, Robert T. and Holland, Winford E., 1978, 'A cross-validation study of the Kirton Adaption Innovation Inventory in three research and development organizations,' *Applied Psychological Measurement*, vol. 2, pp. 563-570.

Kets de Vries, Manfred F. R., 1977, 'The entrepreneurial personality: A person at the crossroads,' *Journal of Management Studies*, vol. 14, no. 1, pp. 34-57.

Kirton, Michael J., 1976, 'Adaptors and innovators: A description and measure,' *Journal of Applied Psychology*, vol. 61, no. 5, pp. 622-629.

Kirton, Michael J., Ed. 1989, Adaptors and innovators: styles of creativity and problem solving, Routledge, London.

Kirton, Michael J., 2003, *Adaption-Innovation: In the context of diversity and change*, Routledge, Hove.

Kirton, Michael J. and McCarthy, Rosalyn M., 1985, 'Personal and group estimates of the Kirton Inventory scores,' *Psychological Reports*, vol. 57, no. 3, pp. 1067-70.

Kohli, Ajay K. and Jaworski, Bernard J., 1990, 'Market orientation: The construct, research propositions, and managerial implications,' *Journal of Marketing*, vol. 54, no. 2, pp. 1-18.

Learned, Edmund Philip, Christensen, C. Roland, Andrews, Kenneth Richmond and Guth, William D., 1965, *Business policy: Text and cases*, Irwin, Homewood.

Lindblom, Charles Edward, 1959, 'The science of muddling through,' *Public Administration Review*, vol. 19, pp. 79-88.

Lindblom, Charles Edward, 1965, *The intelligence of democracy: Decision making through mutual adjustment*, Free Press, New York.

Miles, Raymond E. and Snow, Charles Curtis, 1978, *Organizational strategy, structure and process*, McGraw-Hill, New York.

Miller, Danny, Kets de Vries, Manfred F. R. and Toulouse, Jean-Marie, 1982, 'Top executive locus of control and its relationship to strategy-making, structure, and environment,' *Academy of Management Journal*, vol. 25, no. 2, pp. 237-253.

Miller, Danny and Toulouse, Jean-Marie, 1998, 'Quasi-rational organizational responses: Functional and cognitive sources of strategic simplicity,' *Revue Canadienne des Sciences de l'Administration*, vol. 15, no. 3, pp. 230-240.

Mintzberg, Henry, 1972, 'Research on strategy-making,' *Academy of Management Proceedings*, pp. 90-94.

Mintzberg, Henry, 1977, 'Strategy formulation as a historical process,' *International Studies of Management & Organization*, vol. 7, no. 2, pp. 28-40.

Mintzberg, Henry, 1978, 'Patterns in strategy formation,' *Management Science*, vol. 24, no. 9, pp. 934-948.

Mintzberg, Henry, 1985, 'The organization as political arena,' *Journal of Management Studies*, vol. 22, no. 2, pp. 133-154.

Mintzberg, Henry, 1987, 'Crafting strategy,' *Harvard Business Review*, vol. 65, no. 4, pp. 66-76.

Mintzberg, Henry, 1987a, 'The strategy concept I: Five Ps for strategy,' *California Management Review*, vol. 30, no. 1, pp. 11-25.

Mintzberg, Henry, 1990, 'The Design School: Reconsidering the basic premises of strategy formation,' *Strategic Management Journal*, vol. 11, no. 3, pp. 171-196.

Mintzberg, Henry, 1994, 'The fall and rise of strategic planning,' *Harvard Business Review*, vol. 72, no. 1, pp. 107-114.

Mintzberg, Henry, 1996, 'Learning 1, planning 0,' California Management Review, vol. 38, no. 4, pp. 92-93.

Mintzberg, Henry, Ahlstrand, Bruce and Lampel, Joseph, 1998, *Strategy safari: A guided tour through the wilds of strategic management*, Free Press, New York.

Mitchell, Ronald K., Agle, Bradley R. and Wood, Donna, 1997, 'Toward a theory of stakeholder identification and salience: Defining the principle of who and what really counts,' *Academy of Management Review*, vol. 22, no. 4, pp. 853-886.

Mudd, Samuel, 1996, 'Kirton's A-I theory: Evidence bearing on the style/level and factor composition,' British Journal of Psychology, vol. 87, no. 2, pp. 241-254.

Noble, Charles H., Sinha, Rajiv K. and Kumar, Ajith, 2002, 'Market orientation and alternative strategic orientations: A longitudinal assessment of performance implications,' *Journal of Marketing*, vol. 66, no. 4, pp. 25-39.

Ohmae, Kenichi, 1982, *The mind of the strategist: The art of Japanese business*, McGraw-Hill, New York.

Oliver, Christine and Holzinger, Ingo 2008, 'The effectiveness of strategic political management: A dynamic capabilities framework,' *Academy of Management Review*, vol. 33, no. 2, pp. 496-520.

Pascale, Richard Tanner, 1984, 'Perspectives on strategy: The real story behind Honda's success,' California Management Review, vol. 26, no. 3, pp. 47-72.

Pfeffer, Jeffrey, 1992, *Managing with power: Politics and influence in organizations*, Harvard Business School Press, Boston.

Pfeffer, Jeffrey and Salancik, Gerald R., 1978, *The External Control of Organizations: A Resource Dependence Perspective*, Harper & Row, New York NY.

Porter, Michael Eugene, 1980, *Competitive strategy: Techniques for analyzing industries and competitors*, Free Press, New York.

Porter, Michael Eugene, 1985, *Competitive advantage: Creating and sustaining superior performance*, Free Press, New York.

Porter, Michael Eugene, 1996, 'What is strategy,' *Harvard Business Review*, vol. 74, no. 6, pp. 61-78.

Quinn, James Brian, 1978, 'Strategic change: "Logical incrementalism",' *Sloan Management Review*, vol. 20, no. 1, pp. 7-21.

Quinn, James Brian, 1980, *Strategies for change: Logical incrementalism*, Irwin, Homewood.

Rotter, Julian B., 1966, 'Generalized expectancies for internal versus external control of reinforcement,' *Psychological Monographs: General and Applied*, vol. 80, Whole No. 609, pp. 1-28.

Rumelt, Richard P., 1979, 'Evaluation of strategy: Theory and models', *Strategic management: A new view of business policy and planning*, D. E. Schendel and C. W. Hofer, Little Brown, Boston, pp. 196-212.

Schumpeter, Joseph Alois, 1934, *The theory of economic development*, Harvard University Press, Cambridge.

Schwartz, Shalom H., 1992, 'Universals in the content and structure of values: Theoretical advances and empirical tests in 20 countries', *Advances in experimental social psychology*, M. P. Zanna, Academic Press, San Diego, vol. 25, pp. 1-65.

Selznick, Philip, 1957, *Leadership in administration: A sociological interpretation*, Harper & Row, New York.

Simon, Herbert Alexander, 1957, *Administrative Behavior: A study of decision-making processes in administrative organizations*, Macmillan, New York.

Smith, Adam, 1991, *An inquiry into the nature and causes of the wealth of nations*, Prometheus, Amherst.

Smith, Norman R., 1967, *The entrepreneur and his firm: The relationship between type of man and type of company*, Michigan State University Graduate School of Business Administration, East Lansing.

Spranger, Eduard, 1928, *Types of men: The psychology and ethics of personality*, Niemeyer, Halle.

Sun, Tzu Wu, 1944, *The art of war*, Military Service Publishing Company, Harrisburg.

Taylor, Jennifer A., 1994, 'Stability of schoolchildren's cognitive style: A longitudinal study of the Kirton Adaptation-Innovation Inventory,' Psychological Reports, vol. 74, no. 3, pp. 1008-1010.

Teece, David J., Pisano, Gary and Shuen, Amy, 1997, 'Dynamic capabilities and strategic management,' *Strategic Management Journal*, vol. 18, no. 7, pp. 509-533.

Vancil, Richard F., 1976, 'Strategy formulation in complex organizations,' *Sloan Management Review*, vol. 17, no. 2, pp. 1-18.

Vernon, Philip Ewart and Allport, Gordon Willard, 1931, 'A test for personal values,' *Journal of Abnormal and Social Psychology*, vol. 26, no. 3, pp. 231-248.

Weick, Karl E. and Roberts, Karlene H., 1993, 'Collective mind in organizations: Heedful interrelating on flight decks,' *Administrative Science Quarterly*, vol. 38, no. 3, pp. 357-381.

Wernerfelt, Birger, 1984, 'A resource-based view of the firm,' *Strategic Management Journal*, vol. 5, no. 2, pp. 171-180.

Wrapp, H. Edward, 1967, 'Good managers don't make policy decisions,' *Harvard Business Review*, vol. 45, no. 5, pp. 91-99.

Index

F

G

H

K

L

M

N

O

P

Q

R

S

CPSIA information can be obtained at www.ICGtesting.com
Printed in the USA
BVOW08s1443220713

326624BV00014B/482/P

9 781450 517454